G.M.

Sunshine Devotionals
Devotions for a Purposeful Talk

Glenesha McIntosh

ISBN 979-8-9856703-0-1 (Paperback)
ISBN 979-8-9856703-1-8 (eBook)

Copyright © 2022 by Glenesha McIntosh

All rights reserved. No part of this publication may be reproduced, distributed, or transmitted in any form or by any means-including photocopying, recording, or other electronic or mechanical methods for commercial purposes-without prior written permission of the Author. The only exception is brief quotations in printed reviews.

Author can be contacted via:
www.gmsunshinedevotionals.com

Churches may reproduce portions of this book without the express written permission of the Author, provided the text does not exceed 500 words or 5 percent of the entire book, whichever is less, and that the text is not material quoted from another publisher. When reproducing text from this book, include the following credit line:
"G.M. Sunshine Devotionals – Devotions for a Purposeful Talk, written by Glenesha McIntosh, Used by permission."

Printed in the United States of America

Prologue

Dear Reader,

This Devotional book is the 2nd in the series G.M. Sunshine Devotionals.

Devotions for a Purposeful Talk is truly amazing. It is yet another 52-week devotional, with 6 supporting days of scripture readings relating to each respective devotional, that is simply timeless. God truly has the most inspiring and creative heart, and I am delighted to see his wonders come into fruition through these devotions.

I pray that it will bless you exceptionally throughout your life and your walks and talks with the Lord.

Be blessed,

Foreword by Lyee McIntosh

'He walks with me and talks with me, and he tells me that I am his own.'

I'm reminded of this song when I think about the title of this book, 'Devotions for a Purposeful Talk', written by my wife and mother of our 4 beautiful children. This is the second book in an ongoing series of books to come.

These writings remind me of a time when my wife and I were courting each other. Glenesha and I would meet up for lunch at different places in Sheepshead Bay, Brooklyn. Sometimes to sit, eat and chat at a nice spot or just to grab something on the go.

In the grab-and-go moments, in the beginnings of Summer and Spring, we would always find ourselves walking along the beach, we would walk and talk about anything and everything. It always felt like it was just the two of us. Those were some special walks and talks, even though it was only for a short period of time. Those moments allowed us to cultivate a relationship and a bond that grew into the wonderful family that we enjoy today with our four children.

This is what I believe this book was birthed from, the longing for a greater understanding of each other, and a moment to talk and get closer with our Heavenly Father.
In the midst of all the turmoil and chaos we're faced with in the world today, we should always take time to build and cultivate a deeper closeness with our Heavenly Father. This

should be our longing and desire. So, as we go out and come in with our daily routine, lets always make the time to have a Purposeful Talk with our Father who is concerned about our every need and who can give insight and answers to our deepest desires and questions.

I thank God for my wife, who he has given to me, and pray that this book will help bring you to a space to get deeper and closer to the one who cares for you.

So why not have a talk with God today; A Meaningful & Purposeful one.

God Bless,

Lyee McIntosh

Contents

Part I: 'I Am!' (#'s 1-31)

1. His Workmanship? — 10
2. Good Works — 13
3. The Door — 17
4. Full & Hungry! Part 1 — 20
5. Full & Hungry! Part 2 — 23
6. Living Stone - Chief Cornerstone! — 26
7. Persistence from the Just & the Unjust — 30
8. Built with Suspension — 32
9. Remembering Affliction — 35
10. Soul Preservation — 38
11. Steadfastness brings security — 43
12. Securing victory and the blessing — 47
13. Lean In A Little Closer — 51
14. You are not called to remain where you are! — 55
15. A New Thing — 59
16. Beautiful Feet! — 61
17. Life Everlasting — 66
18. The Life of Freedom — 69
19. Be Present — 72
20. Remembering Mercies, Humbled in Grace, Elevated through Favor — 76
21. The Manual — 82

22. From One to Many!	86
23. Be Wary of Being Weary	89
24. Rainy Outlook	94
25. The Message – Act 1: The Setup	98
26. The Message – Act 2: The Confrontation	101
27. The Message – Act 3: The Resolution	108
28. Concerning Prayer	112
29. Freedom of Choice & the effect on prayer	117
30. All you need is one!	121
31. Best Self!	124

Part II: Talk Of The Tongue (#'s 32-43)

32. Who Do Men Say I Am?	131
33. Just a Little While Longer	138
34. Nothing is Too Hard for God	143
35. Don't Feed the Symptom	146
36. Give Up? … Nah!	150
37. Forgetting Forgiveness?	152
38. Sharing Understanding	156
39. Mature Acceptance	160
40. The Early Bird Catches the Worm	165
41. Speak Up, Not Down	168
42. Edification Speaks	172
43. My Idiosyncrasy!	177

Part III: Control & Affect (#'s 44-52)

44. Concepts to Basis — 183

45. The Shift is Restricted by the Entanglement — 187

46. Peace in the Replacement — 193

47. Life Lesson Moments — 196

48. The Great Multitude — 201

49. Heart Envy — 205

50. Purposeful Love — 210

51. With Wisdom & Love (The Rod) — 213

52. Perfecting Patience — 219

A MESSAGE FROM THE AUTHOR

GUEST WRITER

BIBLIOGRAPHY

Part I

"I AM!"

Devotional #'s 1-31

"And all the trees of the field shall know that I the Lord have brought down the high tree, have exalted the low tree, have dried up the green tree, and have made the dry tree to flourish: I the Lord have spoken and have done it."
Ezekiel 17:24 KJV

Devotional # 1

His Workmanship?

"Do you not know that your bodies are temples of the Holy Spirit, who is in you, whom you have received from God? You are not your own; you were bought at a price. Therefore honor God with your bodies."
1 Corinthians 6:19-20 NIV

Sometimes we get so caught up with being everything to everyone and we forget about ourselves. Although many can identify with this, the effects are not the same for everyone. Some may have spouses, parents, friends, children, grandchildren, etc. that look out for their wellbeing by putting thought and care for that mission-filled person as priority. Others may not have the privilege of someone that's looking out for their best interest, so they can become more depleted than those that do.

Jesus had not just one but 12 disciples. Each looking out for the Lord, whether genuine or not. As followers of Christ, we must also acknowledge the value of the body (the church, including our circles that each play a significant part in our lives). Being anointed or called or even tasked with a purpose should not negate our connection to those bodies. The Bible teaches us that we are our brother's keeper.

Yes, there are many times during the test that you will have to go it alone and only because of the strength of God we did not faint in our depleted state. Likewise, there are many times when God requires our alone time for prayer and relationship, even on a daily basis. This shouldn't be confused with the importance of the body and our dependency to lean on each part/member operating within their function.

Being about God's business is not always easy. It takes strength, focus, determination, and endurance (among other things). But without someone in our corner to say, 'here's some food, you need to eat', or 'you need to drink something, here's some water', or 'take 5 minutes to rest a bit; is there anything I can do to help?'; we'll find that we can easily push ourselves to a point where we neglect the daily consistency of self-care.

Our physical bodies are temples of the Holy Spirit which resides within. And just as we pay attention to our spiritual fruit, we also need to pay attention to our physical fruit and the signs that our bodies give us that indicate a request for attention. Good health is not just a need, it is a requirement to walk the walk effectively, so that when we talk the talk, it is evident that the word of God doesn't just pierce "as far as the division of the soul and spirit [the completeness of a person]", but that it also does the same of both our "joints and marrow [the deepest parts of our nature]". And when God's word has convicted both the spirit and nature of man; it is then that his living, active, operative, energizing and effective word, fully swoops in "exposing and judging the very thoughts and intentions of the heart" (Hebrews 4:12 AMP).

"Dear friend, I pray that you may enjoy good health and that all may go well with you, even as your soul is getting along well." 3 John 1:2 NIV

We are his Workmanship.

1 - Scriptures

Motivate: _____

"I praise you, for I am fearfully and wonderfully made. Wonderful are your works; my soul knows it very well." Psalm 139:14 ESV

Teach: _____

"... present your bodies as a living sacrifice, holy and acceptable to God, which is your spiritual worship." Romans 12:1 ESV

Win: _____

"...holding fast to the Head, from whom the whole body, nourished and knit together through its joints and ligaments, grows with a growth that is from God." Colossians 2:19 ESV

Trust: _____

"And he is the head of the body, the church...." Colossians 1:18 ESV

Fear-Not: _____

"For in one Spirit we were all baptized into one body..." 1 Corinthians 12:13 ESV

Shift: _____

"Heal me, O Lord, and I shall be healed; save me, and I shall be saved, for you are my praise." Jeremiah 17:14 ESV

Devotional # 2

Good Works

The Bible says, "For by grace you have been saved through faith. And this is not your own doing; it is the gift of God, not a result of works, so that no one may boast. For we are his workmanship, created in Christ Jesus for good works, which God prepared beforehand, that we should walk in them."
Ephesians 2:8-10 ESV

When we accept Jesus Christ as our Lord and Savior, we become his workmanship. This means that we become equipped with a level of skill that only he can give us. And the quality of our life and the abilities in which we execute our given tasks, identifies with the greatness of our master teacher and creator.

But what happens when we don't do what is right? The Bible teaches us this lesson very early in the book of Genesis. "If you do what is right, will you not be accepted? But if you do not do what is right, sin is crouching at your door; it desires to have you, but you must rule over it."
Genesis 4:7 NIV

Sin is always stooped outside our door ready to rush in, if we give it the opportunity, by giving into temptation. But if we submit ourselves to God and resist the devil, he will flee. (James 4:7)

Many know the scripture from Acts 16:31 NLT "Believe in the Lord Jesus and you will be saved..."; and many use this as a full stop on what it means to be a Christian. But this verse is only the beginning. This verse is from a story about a jailer or what we would call in modern day times, a correction officer (person in charge of a jail or prisoners in it). The story talks about Paul and Silas casting out a demon from a fortune teller that made her slave masters wealthy, however once the demon was cast out, her masters' hopes of wealth were shattered. They incited an uproar against Paul and Silas on the basis that they were teaching customs that were illegal for Romans to practice. This uproar quickly went wrong when the city officials ordered them to be stripped and beaten and then thrown into prison. But in their imprisonment, they prayed and praised God, and God responded with a massive earthquake that flew open all the doors of the prisoners as well as loosed every chain that were holding them.

The jailer woke up and thought that all the prisoners had escaped and attempted to take his own life, but Paul shouted to him not to do it because they were all still in the prison and had not left. It was then that the jailer fell before Paul and Silas asking what he must do to be saved. The first step that Paul and Silas stated to him was to Believe in the Lord Jesus and he will be saved along with everyone in his household, if they believed as well. The second step was listening to the Word of the Lord. Paul and Silas "shared the word of the Lord with him and with all who lived in his household. Even at that hour of the night, the jailer cared for them and washed their wounds." Acts 16:32-33 NLT. The third step was that the jailer and everyone in his household were baptized.

Baptism signifies the commitment to serve the Lord by the washing away of our sins and being made whole (of one body and spirit of the Lord) which allows us to walk in the newness of life in Christ Jesus, receiving the gift of the Holy Spirit.

When we think about being saved (salvation), we are looking forward to an eternity in the Kingdom of God, and believing in Jesus Christ is only the first step to salvation. Romans 10:16 NKJV says, "faith comes by hearing, and hearing by the word of God". Verse 18 NLT says "The message has gone throughout the earth, and the words to all the world".

Therefore as a part of salvation we have the responsibility of positioning ourselves to where we can hear the word of God being preached. John 3:5-7 NLT confirms the third step by Jesus himself saying "I assure you, no one can enter the Kingdom of God without being born of water and the Spirit. Humans can reproduce only human life, but the Holy Spirit gives birth to spiritual life. So don't be surprised when I say, 'You must be born again'."

As long as we have life, this three-step process of salvation (belief, faith, and walking in newness of a spiritual life birthed through baptism) will continually manifest in our lives if we DO what is right in the eyes of the Lord. Which means that we must follow his lead and direction in order to stay on track every step of the way. James 2:14 ESV says "What good is it, my brothers, if someone says he has faith but does not have works? Can that faith save him?" "For as the body apart from the spirit is dead, so also faith apart from works is dead." James 2:26 ESV.

Visions, dreams, talents, gifts, and so much more are all given to us to do Good Works; Good works that guarantees our acceptance into the Kingdom of God.

2 - Scriptures

Motivate: _____

"Those things, which ye have both learned, and received, and heard, and seen in me, do: and the God of peace shall be with you." Philippians 4:9 KJV

Teach: _____

"*Instruct them* to do good, to be rich in good works, to be generous, willing to share [with others]. ¹⁹ In this way storing up for themselves the *enduring* riches of a good foundation for the future, so that they may take hold of that which is truly life." 1 Timothy 6:18-19 AMP

Win: _____

"But whoever looks intently into the perfect law that gives freedom, and continues in it—not forgetting what they have heard, but doing it—they will be blessed in what they do." James 1:25 NIV

Trust: _____

"And let us not grow weary of doing good, for in due season we will reap, if we do not give up." Galatians 6:9 ESV

Fear-Not: _____

"In the same way, let your light shine before others, so that they may see your good works and give glory to your Father who is in heaven." Matthew 5:16 ESV

Shift: _____

"Whatever you do [whatever your task may be], work from the soul [that is, put in your very best effort], as [something done] for the Lord and not for men," Colossians 3:23 AMP

Devotional # 3

The Door

The Bible mentions doors so many times; Narrow doors, wide doors, open doors, closed doors...

Doors are just a big factor in life, and as much as it's meant for going out and coming in; even more significantly it is only meant to allow access for ONE at a time.

This is similar to how favor works, as it is also meant to allow access for one, and that one is Jesus Christ.

So how do we gain access to that favor if it only grants access to Christ?

To the world, ONE is recognized as singular, but to God, because of the Sacrifice of his son Jesus Christ (the essence of Grace), his body (manifested in the holy spirit) was broken and shared to all who received it. In Matthew 26:26 ESV Jesus said "... Take, eat; this is my body.". Therefore, to God, one is recognized as plural, because all who have received and believe are counted as members of Jesus' ONE body and therefore receives access to the workings of favor. Favor that is the divine act of Grace.

Because of Grace, you don't have to decide who goes first or last, or who gets the opportunity when many meet the eligibility requirements, God decides, through favor.

Favor isn't fair and fair isn't favor.

What does that mean? If you got the job, everyone else didn't. So, do you mope about it daily, saddened about your selection because it meant the rejection of many? No, we rejoice because favor has done its perfect work.

What is considered favor in the body of believers is called lucky to the rest of the world. And likewise, what is considered a lack of favor is the notion of being unlucky.

When Grace is activated, for those who believe in the Lord Jesus Christ, the door of favor functions purposefully, opening and shutting many doors throughout our lives as we move according to God's plan.

But favor doesn't only open and close doors, it also exists as an important element that allows the Grace of God to flow freely and limitlessly in our day-to-day living. Ecclesiastes 10:12 ESV says "The words of a wise man's mouth win him favor, but the lips of a fool consume him." Wow. We may not think that our words can win us favor, but it does. What we say can make us or break us. It can elevate us or bring us down or even keep us where we are. Even the things we say that are overheard by others, can have a significant impact on both our lives and theirs; Children particularly are big factors of that. Ephesians 4:29 ESV says "Let no corrupting talk come out of your mouths, but only such as is good for building up, as fits the occasion, that it may give grace to those who hear." To give Grace is the workings and manifestation of favor.

No matter how you look at it, favor is an essential part of life. Proverbs 22:1 ESV says that "favor is better than silver or gold." Having our faith hinged securely in not only believing that God is real, and in not only taking care of our bodies and members of the body; but, by also putting our trust in the Lord AND doing good, ensures that his favor will be active and applicable to our purpose unto good works, every step of our way.

3 - Scriptures

Motivate: _____

"I am the door. If anyone enters by me, he will be saved and will go in and out and find pasture." John 10:9 ESV

Teach: _____

"For the Lord God is a sun and shield; the Lord bestows favor and honor. No good thing does he withhold from those who walk uprightly." Psalm 84:11 ESV

Win: _____

"Ask, and it will be given to you; seek, and you will find; knock, and it will be opened to you." Matthew 7:7 ESV

Trust: _____

"Let the favor of the Lord our God be upon us, and establish the work of our hands upon us; yes, establish the work of our hands!" Psalm 90:17 ESV

Fear-Not: _____

"And wherever they do not receive you, when you leave that town shake off the dust from your feet as a testimony against them." Luke 9:5 ESV

Shift: _____

"Behold, I stand at the door and knock. If anyone hears my voice and opens the door, I will come in to him and eat with him, and he with me." Revelation 3:20 ESV

Devotional # 4

Full & Hungry! Part 1

I have learned, in whatsoever state I am, therewith to be content. I know both how to be abased, and I know how to abound: every where and in all things I am instructed both to be full and to be hungry, both to abound and to suffer need. I can do all things through Christ which strengtheneth me." Philippians 4:11-13 KJV

The Bible has given us such a great view and perspectives that have opened our eyes to what the Lord truly wants for us.

Whatever situation we're in, the Bible tells us that we should be both full and hungry. But how can we be both at the same time? To be full is to be content, satisfied, happy, sufficient, stuffed, plentiful, filled, and even bursting. It is being in a place of full saturation wherever God has you, **for the time being**. But to be hungry means that you are eager with hope. Romans 15:13 NIV says "May the God of hope fill you with all joy and peace as you trust in him, so that you may **overflow with hope** by the power of the Holy Spirit." So although we are full/content with **where God has us now**, we are hungry/hopeful as we trust in God **for where he is taking us**.

We serve a living God. A God who is ever moving, constantly causing the stories of our lives to fall into place. Believing in him, knowing that where we are is only for a time, hoping for what he has in store for us, and trusting that we will do great things in his name - is essential to our growth in becoming all that we can be.

Jesus said "Very truly I tell you, whoever believes in me will do the works I have been doing, and they will do even greater things than these, because I am going to the Father. And I will do whatever you ask in my name, so that the Father may be glorified in the Son." John 14:12-13 NIV.

This is what strengthens us, our full yet hungry spirit to not only be content in doing the work that Christ did, but to be hungry and hopeful enough to do even greater works because of the benefit of doing all things through him. And in applying ourselves willingly and obediently, the Lord has in turn committed himself to us, in doing whatever we ask for by the power of his name.

4 - Scriptures

Motivate: _____

"The afflicted will eat and be satisfied; Those who [diligently] seek Him and require Him [as their greatest need] will praise the Lord..." Psalm 22:26 AMP

Teach: _____

"But **godliness** with contentment is great gain, for we brought nothing into the world, and we cannot take anything out of the world." 1 Timothy 6:6 ESV

Win: _____

"Now **faith** is the assurance of things hoped for, the conviction of things not seen." Hebrews 11:1 ESV

Trust: _____

"And from his fullness we have all received, grace upon grace." John 1:16 ESV

Fear-Not: _____

"And my God will supply every need of yours according to his riches in glory in Christ Jesus." Philippians 4:19 ESV

Shift: _____

"And all these blessings shall come upon you and overtake you, if you obey the voice of the Lord your God. Blessed shall you be in the city, and blessed shall you be in the field." Deuteronomy 28:2-3 ESV

Devotional # 5

Full & Hungry! Part 2

The scripture, Philippians 4:11-13 instructs us "both to abound and to suffer need". Being full/content and hungry/hopeful can go much deeper than works, our current situation, and where we're going in life. Why? Because whatever we do in the natural is also manifested in the spirit. When we abound, we're more than just filled, we are in overflow and made alive by the spiritual foundation and confession of our faith. In moving in that mode of overflow, it subjects us to continuously suffer need because of the continuous flow of the outpour that we undergo daily. This is why it is vital to be constantly filled. It's like being content with a full tank of gas, but because of the never-ending use when we drive, we are in continuous need to replace what is being emptied.

Therefore, just saying that we're contented with where we are in life or that we're hopeful that things will change (so that we can convince ourselves that God **is** working), is not enough to produce the workings of faith. Our confession of faith is one that is a recurrent cycle, and it is made evident by our good works that should always be full and abound in overflow. At the same time as much as we pour out, we suffer need to be refilled. And that's where the amazing part happens, because it is God who does the pouring out of his spirit so that we are filled. And when we prosper in that filling because of the need produced by the overflow, God's word never returns to him void. Why? Because his word never fails to manifest through our lives, thereby bringing back the glory to the one who did the pouring in the first place.

This makes me think of the cycle of life. Because although we consider that cycle mostly in the natural, the spiritual manifestation of the cycle of life is validated by being both **Full and Hungry**. It is not only based on our current situation or place in life that causes a succession of changes to occur, but it is also based on a spiritual foundation established on the confession of our faith, that through works, <u>we produce a cycle</u> that is **constantly hungry** (while we are pouring out), **always re-filled** (while God is pouring into us), **always manifesting** (while the word accomplishes), **and never coming back void** (because it always brings back glory to God).

5 - Scriptures

Motivate: _____

"The glory that you have given me I have given to them, that they may be one even as we are one," John 17:22 ESV

Teach: _____

"All Scripture is God-breathed [given by divine inspiration] and is profitable for instruction, for conviction [of sin], for correction [of error and restoration to obedience], for training in righteousness [learning to live in conformity to God's will, both publicly and privately—behaving honorably with personal integrity and moral courage]; so that the man of God may be complete *and* proficient, outfitted *and* thoroughly equipped for every good work." 2 Timothy 3:16-17 AMP

Win: _____

"For I was hungry and you gave me food, I was thirsty and you gave me drink, I was a stranger and you welcomed me," Matthew 25:35 ESV

Trust: _____

"Now faith is the assurance of things hoped for, the conviction of things not seen." Hebrews 11:1 ESV

Fear-Not: _____

"So shall My word be that goes forth from My mouth; It shall not return to Me void, But it shall accomplish what I please, And it shall prosper *in the thing* for which I sent it." Isaiah 55:11 NKJV

Shift: _____

"You ask and do not receive, because you ask wrongly, to spend it on your passions." James 4:3 ESV

Devotional # 6

Living Stone - Chief Cornerstone!

[Coming to Him *as to* a living stone, rejected indeed by men, but chosen by God *and* precious, you also, as living stones, are being built up a spiritual house, a holy priesthood, to offer up spiritual sacrifices acceptable to God through Jesus Christ. Therefore it is also contained in the Scripture, **"Behold, I lay in Zion A chief cornerstone, elect, precious, And he who believes on Him will by no means be put to shame."** Therefore, to you who believe, *He is* precious; but to those who are disobedient, **"The stone which the builders rejected Has become the chief cornerstone,"** and **"A stone of stumbling And a rock of offense."** They stumble, being disobedient to the word, to which they also were appointed. But you *are* a chosen generation, a royal priesthood, a holy nation, His own special people, that you may proclaim the praises of Him who called you out of darkness into His marvelous light; who once *were* not a people but *are* now the people of God, who had not obtained mercy but now have obtained mercy.] 1 Peter 2:4-10 NKJV.

That scripture is truly a lot to take in. Have you ever thought that you were a living Stone? The scripture says that Jesus, was chosen by God and precious. He was born and lived among men as a living Stone that was rejected by the same men, who he came to save. Whether we're old or young, we are living stones as well, being built into something great; a spiritual house from the family of the deity of God. Our spiritual sacrifice is our heart that is offered freely to God and it is acceptable to him because of the eternal sacrifice of Jesus.

Through Jesus Christ's death and resurrection, God has shown us that he has laid a Chief cornerstone in Zion, the pinnacle of the promised land, the Kingdom of God. The scripture says, "Then I looked, and there before me was the Lamb, standing on Mount Zion..." Revelation 14:1 NIV. That Chief Cornerstone, the lamb (Jesus), forms the base of our relationship with God, joining us to him. And we depend on Jesus for that important connection; And as long as we trust and believe in him, we will never be put to shame because "If God is for us, who can be against us?" (Romans 8:31 NIV). All who rejects Jesus will see that he is a stone that will cause them to stumble and fall, because they cannot build a relationship with God without acknowledging Jesus as the Chief cornerstone of connection. But for those who accept Jesus and believe in him the bible says "For he will command his angels concerning you to guard you in all your ways; they will lift you up in their hands, **so that you will not strike your foot against a stone**." Psalm 91:11-12 NIV

An important thing to remember is that we are all God's children, which means that whether disobedient or obedient, we were all appointed to the Word of God. After all, we were formed and received the breath of life, so that we can establish dominion over all the **world,** that the **word** has created. Funny thing! If you remove the letter 'l' from the word 'world', you are left with **the '<u>word</u>'**, in which the scripture tells us that we were appointed to. Isn't that amazing! What sets us apart and causes us to become **Children of God** (yes, there is a difference), is that for we who believe or are coming to Christ, the scripture (1 Peter 2:9-10) says that we are considered, "a chosen generation, a royal priesthood, a holy nation, His own special people, that **you may proclaim the praises of Him who called you** out of darkness into His marvelous light; who once *were* not a people but *are* **now the people of God, who had not obtained mercy but now have obtained mercy**".

After rejection, suffering, and bearing all our sins, dying and being raised from the dead; Christ is still advocating for us, day after day, because we are his own. He is embedded in the very living word that our faith is founded and grounded upon, and I am eternally grateful to be a living stone with Christ as the Chief Cornerstone.

6 - *Scriptures*

Motivate: _____

"And I tell you, you are Peter, and on this rock I will build my church, and the gates of hell shall not prevail against it." Matthew 16:18 ESV

Teach: _____

"For there is one God, and there is one mediator between God and men, the man Christ Jesus," 1 Timothy 2:5 ESV

Win: _____

"Don't let anyone capture you with empty philosophies and high-sounding nonsense that come from human thinking and from the spiritual powers of this world, rather than from Christ." Colossians 2:8 NLT

Trust: _____

"See what kind of love the Father has given to us, that we should be called children of God; and so we are. The reason why the world does not know us is that it did not know him." 1 John 3:1 ESV

Fear-Not: _____

"So then you are no longer strangers and aliens, but you are fellow citizens with the saints and members of the household of God, built on the foundation of the apostles and prophets, Christ Jesus himself being the cornerstone," Ephesians 2:19-20 ESV

Shift: _____

"According to the [remarkable] grace of God which was given to me [to prepare me for my task], like a skillful master builder I laid a foundation, and now another is building on it. But each one must be careful how he builds on it," 1 Corinthians 3:10 AMP

Devotional # 7

Persistence from the Just & the Unjust

Now Jesus was telling the disciples a parable to make the point that at all times they ought to pray and not give up and lose heart, saying, "In a certain city there was a judge who did not fear God and had no respect for man. There was a [desperate] widow in that city and she kept coming to him and saying, 'Give me justice and legal protection from my adversary.' For a time he would not; but later he said to himself, 'Even though I do not fear God nor respect man, yet because this widow continues to bother me, I will give her justice and legal protection; otherwise by continually coming she [will be an intolerable annoyance and she] will wear me out.' " Then the Lord said, "Listen to what the unjust judge says! And will not [our just] God defend and avenge His elect [His chosen ones] who cry out to Him day and night? Will He delay [in providing justice] on their behalf? I tell you that He will defend and avenge them quickly. However, when the Son of Man comes, will He find [this kind of persistent] faith on the earth?"

Luke 18:1-8 AMP

7 - *Scriptures*

Motivate: _____

"Pray without ceasing." 1 Thessalonians 5:17 KJV

Teach: _____

"But as for me, I will look expectantly for the Lord and with confidence in Him I will keep watch; I will wait [with confident expectation] for the God of my salvation. My God will hear me." Micah 7:7 AMP

Win: _____

"And let us not be weary in well doing: for in due season we shall reap, if we faint not." Galatians 6:9 KJV

Trust: _____

"Therefore, my beloved brothers, be steadfast, immovable, always abounding in the work of the Lord, knowing that in the Lord your labor is not in vain." 1 Corinthians 15:58 ESV

Fear-Not: _____

"You know we call those blessed [happy, spiritually prosperous, favored by God] who were steadfast and endured [difficult circumstances]. You have heard of the patient endurance of Job and you have seen the Lord's outcome [how He richly blessed Job]. The Lord is full of compassion and is merciful." James 5:11 AMP

Shift: _____

"Keep on asking, and you will receive what you ask for. Keep on seeking, and you will find. Keep on knocking, and the door will be opened to you." Matthew 7:7 NLT

Devotional # 8

Built with Suspension

Resilience is the ability to spring back, bounce back, or recover quickly. Micah 7:8 NIV says "Do not gloat over me, my enemy! Though I have fallen, I will rise. Though I sit in darkness, the Lord will be my light."

How appropriate is this scripture to resilience? "Though I have fallen, I will rise". How many times have we heard people just give up because they didn't succeed the first time or throw in the towel saying it wasn't meant to be? Many of us have even said that the reason why it didn't work out is because of God. I'm not saying that God doesn't have a hand in the workings of our lives, but many of us put it all on God as if we didn't have a hand in the reason things didn't work out.

This scripture teaches us that failure is only temporary. By using the word "I" it draws a great sense of self ownership to failure and an even greater ownership to the responsibility of bouncing back; "I" have fallen, "I" will rise." The scripture further says, though "I" sit in darkness, the Lord will be "my" light. Regardless of the growth that comes with taking ownership, spiritual maturity means that when we find ourselves in a place where we have no control, we can acknowledge the one who does have control, God; And **he will be** everything we cannot. That's when the word "**I**" becomes "**my**". The word "I" is self, but the word "my" gives a belonging to or association with someone or something linking a deeper connection and relationship that enhances the qualities and value of oneself.

Micah 7:9 NIV continues the responsibility of owning our wrong-doing, places where we've fallen short, and also accepting that there will be consequences to actions and situations that we've created. It says "Because **I** have sinned against him, I will bear the Lord's wrath, until he pleads my case and upholds my cause. He will bring me out into the light; I will see his righteousness."

There are lessons we must learn, tests we must pass, dead branches to be shaken off, weak areas we must nurture and strengthen and new sprouts we must grow, all while the Lord grants us Mercy and forgiveness in the journey that brings us out of darkness and into his light.

The scripture tells us that "I" will bear it and the Lord will plead "my" case and uphold "my" cause. Then it draws reference to the responsibility of God by the word "He". "He" will bring me out. This speaks to the faithfulness of God and his promises. So once we have taken responsibility and done our part, then he will do his part, to bring us out. It is "he" who pleads on our behalf and upholds that which is our cause, our purpose, our reason. And when he does what he does, it is we who see his righteousness on our behalf when we couldn't have done it for ourselves.

That is the kind of suspension that we are built with. The ability to bounce back even better than before, to be renewed, rebuilt, restored.

"O give thanks unto the Lord, for he is good: for his mercy endureth for ever. Let the redeemed of the Lord say so, whom he hath redeemed from the hand of the enemy;" Psalms 107:1-2 KJV

8 - Scriptures

Motivate: _____

"Have I not commanded you? Be strong and courageous! Do not be terrified or dismayed (intimidated), for the Lord your God is with you wherever you go." Joshua 1:9 AMP

Teach: _____

"Be assured that the testing of your faith [through experience] produces endurance [leading to spiritual maturity, and inner peace]." James 1:3 AMP

Win: _____

"Do not rejoice over me [amid my tragedies], O my enemy! Though I fall, I will rise; Though I sit in the darkness [of distress], the Lord is a light for me." Micah 7:8 AMP

Trust: _____

"I will bear the indignation and wrath of the Lord Because I have sinned against Him, Until He pleads my case and executes judgment for me. He will bring me out to the light, And I will behold His [amazing] righteousness and His remarkable deliverance." Micah 7:9 AMP

Fear-Not: _____

"For I will restore health unto thee, and I will heal thee of thy wounds, saith the LORD; because they called thee an Outcast, saying, This is Zion, whom no man seeketh after." Jeremiah 30:17 KJV

Shift: _____

"He restoreth my soul." Psalm 23:3 KJV

Devotional # 9

Remembering Affliction

"Remembering mine affliction and my misery, the wormwood and the gall. My soul hath them still in remembrance, and is humbled in me. This I recall to my mind, therefore have I hope. It is of the Lord's mercies that we are not consumed, because his compassions fail not. They are new every morning: great is thy faithfulness. The Lord is my portion, saith my soul; therefore will I hope in him. The Lord is good unto them that wait for him, to the soul that seeketh him." Lamentations 3:19-25 KJV

Afflictions are something that many try to forget. But as much as we try to wipe them out of our memory, the Bible tells us that our soul remembers them. And because our soul remembers them, God has a constant reminder of our afflictions. I am humbled because I cannot hide from God. He sees all, he knows all, and when I think about these things, I remember how much God cares for me and loves me. This gives me hope.

We put our hope in the Lord because not only does he know where we've been, but he knows where we're going. Who can we put our hope in, that is greater than the Lord? He has forgiven us over and over again by giving us his mercy so that we are not consumed by our sin. His kindness and love towards us is so great, who can compare? When a child is born, as they grow they can resemble so many different members of our family, but to God, we (his children) are a direct reflection of him at all times because he made us in his own image.

Our soul holds onto God because, it doesn't die. It is an extension of God. The Bible says, "And the Lord God formed man of the dust of the ground, and breathed into his nostrils the breath of life; and man became a living soul." Genesis 2:7 KJV. We not only received the breath of life, but we became a living eternal soul that is not bound to this earth. "The Lord is my portion, saith my soul; therefore will I hope in him." Lamentations 3:24 KJV

We wait for the Lord because our soul continually seeks that which is its portion. And God is good to them that wait.

9 - Scriptures

Motivate: _____

"Here is [encouragement for] the steadfast endurance of the saints (God's people), those who habitually keep God's commandments and their faith in Jesus." Revelation 14:12 AMP

Teach: _____

"No temptation has overtaken you except such as is common to man; but God is faithful, who will not allow you to be tempted beyond what you are able, but with the temptation will also make the way of escape, that you may be able to bear it." 1 Corinthians 10:13 NKJV

Win: _____

"Many are the afflictions of the righteous: but the Lord delivereth him out of them all." Psalm 34:19 KJV

Trust: _____

"It is good for me that I have been afflicted; that I might learn thy statutes." Psalm 119:71 KJV

Fear-Not: _____

"And we know that all things work together for good to those who love God, to those who are the called according to *His* purpose." Romans 8:28 NKJV

Shift: _____

"For He has not despised nor detested the suffering of the afflicted; Nor has He hidden His face from him; But when he cried to Him for help, He listened." Psalm 22:24 AMP

Devotional # 10

Soul Preservation

The cell phone can be considered as an important part of our daily lives. In fact, many can't even function on a day-to-day basis without it. Over the years it has fluctuated greatly in design, flexibility, and accessibility, and customized to fit seamlessly into the life and style of many. It is what many can consider as a freedom of expression as well as a connectivity to much that life has to offer. But as attractive and functional as a cell phone can be, it is not independently functional without certain key aspects of operation.

A cell phone is just a thing, a body, a shell, if it is not usable. It can't make calls, connect with others, or send and receive messages or information. In order for it to be functional it needs to be connected to a network. That Network is like our spirit. *The bible says in James 2:26 that' the body apart from the spirit is dead'.* But we can't leave the provider out, because it is the provider who provides access to the network so that the cell phone can receive that service. But there is still one more element that makes this whole experience possible; and that's a SIM card.

A SIM card, that is received from a Provider, gives your phone its identity, establishing a belonging to the Provider that is safely secured in the core of its being. Not only does it identify solely to the Provider, it is the thing that enables the phone and the Provider the ability to communicate via the network. It also stores valuable data and information throughout the life of the phone.

Our soul is like that of a sim card; it belongs to God our creator, who has safely secured it until that day. Ezekiel 18:4 KJV says "Behold, all souls are mine..."

As our provider, God, has breathed into us the breath of life (his spirit), so that we can be a living being (Genesis 2:7), and not just a body.

The Spirit, according to Isaiah 11:2, is the wisdom, understanding, counsel, might, knowledge and fear of the Lord. It is the spirit of the Lord that has the power to place life into something that is considered lifeless (like dirt), and form something new (man), and give it the ability to bear fruit (multiply). Our spirit is the portion of the Spirit of God that was breathed into us forming the reality of our existence (confirming truth) and an earthly spiritual being that gives us a freedom that allows us to choose whom we will accept, believe in, and serve, thereby allowing us to have a Holy Spirit or an Evil Spirit. No matter the free spirit we possess, we have a soul (a sealed spirit) that belongs to the Lord, residing in a realm that holds our fate. It silently captures and bears witness of how we've lived our earthly lives, that patiently waits for our immortal judgment and eternal life.

Our soul is our hidden spiritual being that is reflective of our current physical being. Throughout the bible we can see just how reflective it can be.

> *3 John 1:2 AMP says "Beloved, I pray that in every way you may succeed and prosper and be in good health [physically], just as [I know] your soul prospers [spiritually]". Proverbs 16:24 AMP says "Pleasant words are like a honeycomb, Sweet and delightful to the soul and healing to the body." Now*

> *when Jeremiah so deeply conveyed his affliction in the Bible, Lamentations 3:17 said that his soul was cast far away from peace. Psalm 142 is a prayer in times of trouble, it says in verse 6-7 AMP "Give attention to my cry, For I am brought very low; Rescue me from my persecutors, For they are stronger than I. Bring my soul out of prison (adversity), So that I may give thanks and praise Your name;...". Even when Jesus was fortelling of his death, he said in John 12:27 AMP "Now My soul is troubled and deeply distressed; what shall I say? 'Father, save Me from this hour [of trial and agony]'?"*

Our soul feels what we go through, it is uplifted when we are uplifted, it prospers when we prosper, and is troubled when we are in distress.

So while our soul waits for the coming of Jesus, and spends it's time retrieving the valuable state of our lives, we ought to preserve the wellbeing of our souls. How do we do that? By having faith and not turning back to a life without Christ.

Hebrews 10:35-39 AMP says "Do not, therefore, fling away your [fearless] confidence, for it has a glorious and great reward. For you have need of patient endurance [to bear up under difficult circumstances without compromising], so that when you have carried out the will of God, you may receive and enjoy to the full what is promised. For yet in a very little while, He who is coming will come, and will not delay. But My righteous one [the one justified by faith] shall live by faith [respecting man's relationship to God and trusting Him]; And if he draws back [shrinking in fear], My soul has no delight in him. **But our way is not that of those who** shrink back to destruction, but [we are] of those who believe [relying on God through faith in Jesus Christ, the Messiah] and by this confident faith preserve the soul."

10 - Scriptures

Motivate: _____

"Truly my soul waiteth upon God: from him cometh my salvation". Psalm 62:1 KJV

Teach: _____

"And thou shalt love the Lord thy God with all thine heart, and with all thy soul, and with all thy might." Deuteronomy 6:5 KJV

Win: _____

"Bless the Lord, O my soul: and all that is within me, bless his holy name. Bless the Lord, O my soul, and forget not all his benefits." Psalm 103:1-2 KJV

Trust: _____

"Because thou wilt not leave my soul in hell, neither wilt thou suffer thine Holy One to see corruption." Acts 2:27 KJV

Fear-Not: _____

"And fear not them which kill the body, but are not able to kill the soul: but rather fear him which is able to destroy both soul and body in hell." Matthew 10:28 KJV

Shift: _____

"O God, You are my God; Early will I seek You; My soul thirsts for You;" Psalm 63:1 NKJV

Devotional # 11

Steadfastness brings security

The faithful love of the Lord never ends! His mercies never cease. Great is His faithfulness; His mercies begin afresh each morning. I say to myself, "The Lord is my inheritance; therefore, I will hope in Him!" Lamentations 3: 22 – 24 (NLT)

Love is the only sure foundation that never ends. Steadfastness is the quality of being dutifully firm and resolute. You cannot win without steadfastness, especially in the last days when we are faced with all measures of adversities. God's love never fails. The truth is, God is love and the steadfast love of the Lord never ceases.

Let's look closer at the word steadfast. It can be interchanged with words like, immovable, unwavering, faithful, or a secure foundation. What foundation? The foundation of God's love. Every relationship must be built upon a foundation of true love. Without this main ingredient, we will live in a constant state of panic due to uncertainty. Are you awaiting the eruption of an earthquake due to shaky grounds? In the natural, foundations that are secure are not made of sand. If so, you will be sinking fast. Natural disasters like a hurricane, tsunami, or the swirling wind due to a whirlwind or tornado will suddenly destroy everything in its path. But when your foundation is securely built on the solid rock – God, you have the assurance of His unfailing love.

An American psychologist and philosopher, Abraham Maslow collected research data over decades of studies.

Maslow's Hierarchy of Needs, conducted on an assessment on the most critical needs that exist among mankind, has often been represented in a hierarchical pyramid with five levels. However, the second and third levels are considered the need for Safety and Belongingness. Safety includes security of possessions, environment, employment, resources, health, property, and other general safety concerns. A sense of belongingness stems from the love and intimacy you share within friendships, family, marriage, and other relationships.

No matter the type of relationship, there will be times of testing, but true love is steadfast, endures forever and will bring security. Being in a constant state of knowing God's love is real, causes us to remain rooted, grounded, and confident in Him.

The most priceless gift God gave us was His son, Jesus. This was done as an expression of His love. Remember John 3:16, For God so loved the world…. It validates that the absolute best gift one can give, during their lifetime here on earth, is love. And long after your departure, people will remember your impact. That is the only reason why Jesus asked us to love one another.

Let us never forget the importance of cultivating security and the need for belongingness. The only thing you owe your fellow brethren is steadfast love. Through your trials, you must remain steadfast and know that "this light momentary affliction is preparing for us an eternal weight of glory beyond all comparison." 2 Corinthians 4:17 ESV

Tinasha Gray

11 - Scriptures

Motivate: _____

"And so, we know and rely on the love God has for us. God is love. Whoever lives in love lives in God, and God in them. This is how love is made complete among us so that we will have confidence on the day of judgment: In this world we are like Jesus. There is no fear in love. But perfect love drives out fear, because fear has to do with punishment. The one who fears is not made perfect in love." 1 John 4:16-18 NIV

Teach: _____

"As the Father has loved me, so have I loved you. Now remain in my love. If you keep my commands, you will remain in my love, just as I have kept my Father's commands and remain in his love." John 15:9-10 NIV

Win: _____

"But you, O Lord, are a God merciful and gracious, slow to anger and abounding in steadfast love and faithfulness." Psalms 86:15 ESV

Trust: _____

"God, being rich in mercy, because of the great love with which he loved us, even when we were dead in our trespasses, made us alive together with Christ - by grace you have been saved" Ephesians 2:4-5 ESV

Fear-Not: _____

"See what kind of love the Father has given to us, that we should be called children of God; and so we are. The reason why the world does not know us is that it did not know him." 1 John 3:1 ESV

Shift: _____

"My command is this: Love each other as I have loved you. Greater love has no one than this: to lay down one's life for one's friends." John 15:12-13 NIV

Devotional # 12

Securing victory and the blessing

Then he called for Moses and Aaron by night, and said, "Rise, go out from among my people, both you and the children of Israel. And go, serve the Lord as you have said. Also take your flocks and your herds, as you have said, and be gone; and bless me also." Exodus 12:31-32 (NKJV)

How do one secure victory and the blessing? Well, from the beginning of time, we see people of all walks of life avidly pursuing a blessed and victorious life. Even countries, cities and families aspire to have a rotunda or in some cases a replica, just to reflect growth, security, and prosperity. If you read the constitution's preamble of the United States, you will see a part that speaks clearly to securing victory and the blessing. "We the People of the United States, in Order to form a more perfect Union, establish Justice, ensure domestic Tranquility, provide for the common defense, promote the general Welfare, and secure the Blessings of liberty to ourselves and our Posterity, do ordain and establish this Constitution for the United States of America."

All throughout scripture, we witness individuals like Pharaoh, Esau, Jacob, Jabez, and many others who sought to secure victory and the blessing. Scripture tells us that Jacob fought for the blessing even though he was already blessed. Listen to this dialogue between Jacob and the angel. And He said, "Let Me go, for the day breaks." But he said, "I will not let You go unless You bless me!" Genesis 32:26.

Well, I have good news for you. Victory belongs to the ones who are abiding in Jesus. As a matter of fact, you are already crowned as a victor, overcomer, and the triumphant one, only if you have made Jesus the Lord and master of your life.

The blessed life is simply the opposite of the cursed life. The blessing can be thought of as your ultimate inheritance. It is the benefits that are associated with your personal relationship with Jesus – The True Blessing. Therefore, as a joint heir to the throne, you must remain faithfully connected to the blesser. Look at the legacies of those in Hebrews 11 as the faith-filled ones who sought after God. That is essentially how victory and the blessing will be secured. Do you remember Jesus calling out the crowd in John 6:26? They were seeking the blessing rather than the blesser. But if you Love God with every fiber of your being, you will not be disappointed.

Tinasha Gray

12 - Scriptures

Motivate:

"Finally, all of you be of one mind, having compassion for one another; love as brothers, be tenderhearted, be courteous; not returning evil for evil or reviling for reviling, but on the contrary blessing, knowing that you were called to this, that you may inherit a blessing. For "He who would love life and see good days, let him refrain his tongue from evil, and his lips from speaking deceit." 1 Peter 3:8-10 NKJV

Teach:

"Jesus answered them and said, "Most assuredly, I say to you, you seek Me, not because you saw the signs, but because you ate of the loaves and were filled. Do not labor for the food which perishes, but for the food which endures to everlasting life, which the Son of Man will give you, because God the Father has set His seal on Him." Then they said to Him, "What shall we do, that we may work the works of God?" Jesus answered and said to them, "This is the work of God, that you believe in Him whom He sent." John 6:26-29 (NKJV)

Win:

"And Jabez called on the God of Israel saying, "Oh, that You would bless me indeed, and enlarge my territory, that Your hand would be with me, and that You would keep me from evil, that I may not cause pain!" So God granted him what he requested." 1 Chronicles 4:10 NKJV

Trust: _____

"For the eyes of the Lord are on the righteous, and His ears are open to their prayers; but the face of the Lord is against those who do evil." 1 Peter 3:12 NKJV

Fear-Not: _____

"For the grace of God has appeared that offers salvation to all people. It teaches us to say "No" to ungodliness and worldly passions, and to live self-controlled, upright and godly lives in this present age, while we wait for the blessed hope—the appearing of the glory of our great God and Savior, Jesus Christ, who gave himself for us to redeem us from all wickedness and to purify for himself a people that are his very own, eager to do what is good." Titus 2:11-14 NIV

Shift: _____

"Submit yourselves, then, to God. Resist the devil, and he will flee from you. Come near to God and he will come near to you." James 4:7-8 NIV

Devotional # 13

Lean In A Little Closer

Psalm 23:1-2 AMP says, "The Lord is my Shepherd [to feed, to guide and to shield me], I shall not want. He lets me lie down in green pastures; He leads me beside the still and quiet waters."

Still waters are usually a part of a stream that is steady in supply, yet constantly renewed. And streams are often found in valleys, flowing from one end of the valley to the other. In fact, most valleys are formed from the erosion of rivers or streams over a long period of time. And even though the surface of many streams may appear to be calm and still; underneath the waters are still flowing, still moving, still carving its way through the earth.

Like the still waters, sometimes we think that the hand of the Lord is not moving, but he is always working under the surface - shaping the course of our way.

Whenever we're feeling relaxed, comfortable, and at-ease, and when we're in a place of green pastures there is an indication of still water. Still waters let us know that the Lord has brought us from the patchy, uncertain grounds and have allowed us to come into a place of peace, serenity, and provision, where we can rest in certainty, security and safety, and in a place where he can feed us unhindered and limitlessly.

Something that's really significant and worth pointing out, is our awareness. Being aware that we are in that place is just as important as being there. When God has made all those provisions to purposefully position us and bring us to that place; If we become unfocused, lax, distracted, and absent-minded, even though we know the Lord's presence is there, we can be unconscious of the leading of our great Shepherd, and we can miss the purpose of why he has lead us into this place, mistaking the valley for our destination.

Psalm 23:3 (AMP) tells us that while he is leading us besides the still waters "He refreshes and restores my soul (life);..." That's it. That's why we are in that place; for a refreshing and restoration. Have you ever been refreshed and restored in the midst of chaos and trouble? How about in the midst of sadness, hostility, suppression and depression?

Regardless of what you've been through, you have come to the right place; and there has never been a greater time for being refreshed and restored. Now is the time. The time for refreshing, the time for restoring, the time for renewing. Now is the time for new ideas, new growth. New energy. Now is the time, to shake off all negativity and everything that held us back. Now is the time to pay attention to things that you have been putting off, to areas of your life that you have neglected. Now is the time to turn the soil and start planting new seeds in our lives. Now is the time to lean in a little bit closer.

As a Shepherd the Lord desires an intimate relationship with us. One that is so close that we can hear his voice within ourselves. He knows us so well that he is always one step ahead of us. He's always available to reach out to us, to nudge us, and to calm the seas so that we can rest. But when we lean in a little closer, we can hear his whispers, we can feel his heart and all the love that he has lavished on us. We can receive what he has for us, and we can embrace his will that he has set before us.

If you read Psalm 23 further the Lord tells us how he will keep us as day turns to night; and how he will not leave our side, ensuring that the sun will always rise again and that we will be uplifted, anointed and overflowing with his great love, blessings, gifts, talents and favor all of our days. When we lean in a little closer, we show God that we want to hear him, that we're interested in him, and that we don't want to miss a moment with him. We show him that we are attentive to his word and to his presence.

So as you walk besides the still waters, as he refreshes and restores your soul (your life), Lean In a Little Closer.

13 - Scriptures

Motivate: _____

"He maketh me to lie down in green pastures: he leadeth me beside the still waters." Psalm 23:2 KJV

Teach: _____

"But whosoever drinketh of the water that I shall give him shall never thirst; but the water that I shall give him shall be in him a well of water springing up into everlasting life." John 4:14 KJV

Win: _____

"For I will pour water upon him that is thirsty, and floods upon the dry ground: I will pour my spirit upon thy seed, and my blessing upon thine offspring" Isaiah 44:3 KJV

Trust: _____

"He that believeth on me, as the scripture hath said, out of his belly shall flow rivers of living water." John 7:38 KJV

Fear-Not: _____

"Therefore with joy shall ye draw water out of the wells of salvation." Isaiah 12:3 KJV

Shift: _____

"And the Lord will continually guide you, And satisfy your soul in scorched and dry places, And give strength to your bones; And you will be like a watered garden, And like a spring of water whose waters do not fail." Isaiah 58:11 AMP

Devotional # 14

You are not called to remain where you are!

"for He delivered us and saved us and called us with a holy calling [a calling that leads to a consecrated life—a life set apart—a life of purpose], not because of our works [or because of any personal merit—we could do nothing to earn this], but because of His own purpose and grace [His amazing, undeserved favor] which was granted to us in Christ Jesus before the world began [eternal ages ago]," 2 Timothy 1:9 AMP

God has a purpose and a plan for our lives and it is not to remain where we are. His plans are to give us a good future and a hope (Jeremiah 29:11). And although the life of purpose that he has set apart for us was not earned because of our works, he knows that because he has given us a mind of our own and freedom to use it, that we would have dreams, desires, aspirations and plans. So he asks that if we want his blessing and for him to establish our plans, that we should commit our works to him (Proverbs 16:3).

Isn't it amazing that the God of all creation has not only set aside a life for us and great plans for us but he gives us the privilege to include our desires in our future as well? Psalm 37:4-7 AMP says "Delight yourself in the Lord , And He will give you the desires and petitions of your heart. Commit your way to the Lord; Trust in Him also and He will do it. He will make your righteousness [your pursuit of right standing with God] like the light, And your judgment like [the shining of] the noonday [sun]. Be still before the Lord; wait patiently for Him and entrust yourself to Him; Do not fret (whine, agonize) because of him who prospers in his way, Because of the man who carries out wicked schemes." Psalms 37:4-7 AMP

When we commit our way to God, it means that we are walking in his light, obeying his statutes, following his precepts, bearing fruits of his spirit. So when it comes to our desires, God is for us and not against us, because we are for him. God is a God of precise timing, so patience and complete trust is required. Can we take the time to be still before the Lord, not comparing our lives and what God is doing with the prosperity of others? Do we believe that we will not remain where we are but that God will lead us forward and will do mighty things in due time if we trust in him?

If you believe that then say Amen, because it is already done.

> ["For as the heavens are higher than the earth, So are My ways higher than your ways, And My thoughts than your thoughts. "For as the rain comes down, and the snow from heaven, And do not return there, But water the earth, And make it bring forth and bud, That it may give seed to the sower And bread to the eater, So shall My word be that goes forth from My mouth; It shall not return to Me void, But it shall accomplish what I please, And it shall prosper in the thing for which I sent it.] Isaiah 55:9-11 NKJV

14 - Scriptures

Motivate: _____

"Therefore I say to you, do not worry about your life, what you will eat or what you will drink; nor about your body, what you will put on. Is not life more than food and the body more than clothing? Look at the birds of the air, for they neither sow nor reap nor gather into barns; yet your heavenly Father feeds them. Are you not of more value than they?" Matthew 6:25-26 NKJV

Teach: _____

Then Job answered the Lord and said, "I know that You can do all things, And that no thought or purpose of Yours can be restrained." Job 42:1-2 AMP

Win: _____

"[You said to me] 'Who is this that darkens and obscures counsel [by words] without knowledge?' Therefore [I now see] I have [rashly] uttered that which I did not understand, Things too wonderful for me, which I did not know." Job 42:3 AMP

Trust: _____

"Trust in the Lord with all thine heart; and lean not unto thine own understanding. In all thy ways acknowledge him, and he shall direct thy paths." Proverbs 3:5-6 KJV

Fear-Not: _____

"I will instruct thee and teach thee in the way which thou shalt go: I will guide thee with mine eye." Psalm 32:8 KJV

Shift: _____

"Remember the former things of old: for I am God, and there is none else; I am God, and there is none like me, Declaring the end from the beginning, and from ancient times the things that are not yet done, saying, My counsel shall stand, and I will do all my pleasure" Isaiah 46:9-10 KJV

Devotional # 15

A New Thing

"Behold, I will do a new thing; now it shall spring forth; shall ye not know it? I will even make a way in the wilderness, and rivers in the desert." Isaiah 43:19 KJV

God is in the business of doing new things in our lives. This means changes are continuously going to happen and growth is an essential part of change.

Change and growth is evident to all, it is not hidden; so **you will know** when God is moving. Even when you feel you are in a place where provision seems scarce and you feel surrounded by untamed chaos or dry continuous circumstances - where every day is just more of the same. God will make a way. He will make provisions. He will bring change. He will bring growth.

Establish your foundation in him, knowing that wherever he takes you, whatever changes happen in your life, that you are grounded in him and that he is your stability.

15 - Scriptures

Motivate:

"This Book of the Law shall not depart from your mouth, but you shall read [and meditate on] it day and night, so that you may be careful to do [everything] in accordance with all that is written in it; for then you will make your way prosperous, and then you will be successful." Joshua 1:8 AMP

Teach:

"We know that our old self [our human nature without the Holy Spirit] was nailed to the cross with Him, in order that our body of sin might be done away with, so that we would no longer be slaves to sin." Romans 6:6 AMP

Win:

"They are created now [called into being by the prophetic word] and not long ago; …" Isaiah 48:7 AMP

Trust:

"You have heard [these things foretold]; look at all this [that has been fulfilled]. And you, will you not declare it?" Isaiah 48:6 AMP

Fear-Not:

"… I proclaim to you [specific] new things from this time, Even hidden things which you have not known." Isaiah 48:6 AMP

Shift:

"and put on the new self [the regenerated and renewed nature], created in God's image, [godlike] in the righteousness and holiness of the truth [living in a way that expresses to God your gratitude for your salvation]." Ephesians 4:24 AMP

Devotional # 16

Beautiful Feet!

"I proclaim your saving acts in the great assembly; I do not seal my lips, Lord, as you know. I do not hide your righteousness in my heart; I speak of your faithfulness and your saving help. I do not conceal your love and your faithfulness from the great assembly." Psalms 40:9-10 NIV

God has done so many great things in our lives and it is meant for the building up and edification of the church, the great assembly which includes anyone who has ears to hear about the goodness of God.

There are so many people secretly going through what you went through, and they have no one to talk to or no one to mentor, guide or counsel them. What if the Bible didn't exist and there were no stories and testimonies of how God made a way out of no way and how God moved on behalf of the people; Of how he performed miracles and healing. Would you be hopeful that he could do the same in your situation if you had never heard the good news?

Good News! That's what it is.

The Bible says, "How beautiful on the mountains are the feet of those who bring good news, who proclaim peace, who bring good tidings, who proclaim salvation, who say to Zion, "Your God reigns!" (Isaiah 52:7 NIV)

It means that you've climbed your mountains and no matter how hard it was, you made it to the top and made a joyful noise. You spoke peace, you let out a high note of praise to

God. You proclaimed that God is a deliverer. How beautiful is that great news.

The Bible says, speak of it, proclaim of his goodness. Don't seal your lips. Don't hide your steadfastness, your perseverance, your hope, your faith. All of that is accounted unto your righteousness and God's love and faithfulness. Don't hide it. If you do then others won't know of the experiences of God's people.

These things that we speak are spiritual realities. We don't just live meaningless lives and attribute everything to luck or misfortune. Rather, we attribute everything we do, say and experience by the Grace and Mercies extended to us to the Glory of God. So our realities are not just worldly realities, they are spiritual realities and they are especially precious to those who have the spirit of God. The bible says, "The person without the Spirit does not accept the things that come from the Spirit of God but considers them foolishness, and cannot understand them because they are discerned only through the Spirit." (1 Corinthians 2:14 NIV). "For the message of the cross is foolishness to those who are perishing, but to us who are being saved it is the power of God." (1 Corinthians 1:18 NIV).

Our messages, our testimonies, are the power of God to the Assembly. Allow God's power to flow freely among the great assembly, so that others may gain strength. We should never be ashamed of our tests and trials that comes to make us stronger and more mature. Rather use the impact of our testing to gauge the level of our spiritual maturity and the significance of our growth.

"O give thanks unto the Lord, for he is good: for his mercy endureth for ever. Let the redeemed of the Lord say so, whom he hath redeemed from the hand of the enemy." Psalm 107:1-2 KJV

16 - Scriptures

Motivate: _____

"And I tell you, everyone who acknowledges me before men, the Son of Man also will acknowledge before the angels of God," Luke 12:8 ESV

Teach: _____

"For we did not follow cleverly devised myths when we made known to you the power and coming of our Lord Jesus Christ, but we were eyewitnesses of his majesty." 2 Peter 1:16 ESV

Win: _____

"One generation shall commend your works to another, and shall declare your mighty acts. On the glorious splendor of your majesty, and on your wondrous works, I will meditate. They shall speak of the might of your awesome deeds, and I will declare your greatness. They shall pour forth the fame of your abundant goodness and shall sing aloud of your righteousness." Psalm 145:4-7 ESV

Trust: _____

"And they have conquered him by the blood of the Lamb and by the word of their testimony, for they loved not their lives even unto death." Revelation 12:11 ESV

Fear-Not: _____

"But you are a chosen race, a royal priesthood, a holy nation, a people for his own possession, that you may proclaim the excellencies of him who called you out of darkness into his marvelous light." 1 Peter 2:9 ESV

Shift: _____

"Therefore do not be ashamed of the testimony about our Lord …" 2 Timothy 1:8 ESV

Devotional # 17

Life Everlasting

I will not die but live, and will proclaim what the Lord has done. Psalms 118:17 NIV

For God so loved the world, that he gave his only begotten Son, that whosoever believeth in him should not perish, but have everlasting life. John 3:16 KJV

If you declare with your mouth, "Jesus is Lord", and believe in your heart that God raised him from the dead, you will be saved. For it is with your heart that you believe and are justified, and it is with your mouth that you profess your faith and are saved. As Scripture says, "Anyone who believes in him will never be put to shame". For there is no difference between Jew and Gentile - the same Lord is Lord of all and richly blesses all who call on him, for, "Everyone who calls on the name of the Lord will be saved". Romans 10:9-13 NIV

Do your best to present yourself to God as one approved, a worker who does not need to be ashamed and who correctly handles the word of truth. 2 Timothy 2:15 NIV

And whatever you do, whether in word or in deed, do it all in the name of the Lord Jesus, giving thanks to God the Father through him. Colossians 3:17 NIV

For I am convinced that neither death nor life, neither angels nor demons, neither the present nor the future, nor any powers, neither height nor depth, nor anything else in all creation, will be able to separate us from the love of God that is in Christ Jesus our Lord. Romans 8:38-39 NIV

17 - Scriptures

Motivate: _____

"When the ground soaks up the falling rain and bears a good crop for the farmer, it has God's blessing. But if a field bears thorns and thistles, it is useless. The farmer will soon condemn that field and burn it." Hebrews 6:7-8 NLT

Teach: _____

Jesus said to him, "I am the [only] Way [to God] and the [real] Truth and the [real] Life; no one comes to the Father but through Me." John 14:6 AMP

Win: _____

"Not everyone who calls out to me, 'Lord! Lord!' will enter the Kingdom of Heaven. Only those who actually do the will of my Father in heaven will enter." Matthew 7:21 NLT

Trust: _____

"I do not ignore or nullify the [gracious gift of the] grace of God [His amazing, unmerited favor], for if righteousness comes through [observing] the Law, then Christ died needlessly. [His suffering and death would have had no purpose whatsoever.]" Galatians 2:21 AMP

Fear-Not: _____

"For sin will no longer be a master over you, since you are not under Law [as slaves], but under [unmerited] grace [as recipients of God's favor and mercy]." Romans 6:14 AMP

Shift: _____

"So let us stop going over the basic teachings about Christ again and again. Let us go on instead and become mature in our understanding.

Surely we don't need to start again with the fundamental importance of repenting from evil deeds and placing our faith in God." Hebrews 6:1 NLT

Devotional # 18

The Life of Freedom

Peace - Freedom from disturbance. The ability to be calm. The desire to be on one accord. The beginning of friendship. Reconciliation of wrong. Agreeing to be neutral. Forming a treaty or a union. The underlying, silent, and many times overlooked word that validates love.

Peace.

Who wants peace but has a heart filled with anger and resentment? Who is starved of peace while silenced in an environment that stifles love? Who has peace but is naive to the turmoil of others that hinders the basis of appreciation?

Words are often spoken before we understand. Choices are often made before clarity is revealed. Actions are often done before meditating on our thoughts. Emotions often erupt before confidence is secure.

John 14:27 NLT says "I am leaving you with a gift—peace of mind and heart. And the peace I give is a gift the world cannot give. So don't be troubled or afraid."

Peace is a gift. The world may misunderstand it as something that has to be taken, requested, demanded, divided equally, or fought for - to be acquired. But the peace of God is given freely to those who believe in Jesus Christ and receive the Holy Spirit who comforts, balances, stabilizes, and fulfills the inner being of the mind and heart with the acknowledgement that you are loved beyond any form of commitment or enjoyment that the world can ever offer you.

You are loved so much that the Lord mentions your name daily without failure.

This gift is a birthright that is bestowed on you as a born again believer if the gospel of Christ; and when it resides within you, you don't have to look for it. It's yours and the world does not have the authority nor the power to take it away from you.

So don't just talk the talk of freedom and walk the walk for freedom, but live the life of Freedom through the tri-unity of Peace (Holy Spirit), Love (God the father), and Grace (Jesus Christ).

18 - Scriptures

Motivate:

"But whenever someone turns to the Lord, the veil is taken away." 2 Corinthians 3:16 NLT

Teach:

"For the Lord is the Spirit, and wherever the Spirit of the Lord is, there is freedom." 2 Corinthians 3:17 NLT

Win:

"So all of us who have had that veil removed can see and reflect the glory of the Lord. ..." 2 Corinthians 3:18 NLT

Trust:

"It is God's will that your honorable lives should silence those ignorant people who make foolish accusations against you." 1 Peter 2:15 NLT

Fear-Not:

"Peace I leave with you; My [perfect] peace I give to you; not as the world gives do I give to you. Do not let your heart be troubled, nor let it be afraid. [Let My perfect peace calm you in every circumstance and give you courage and strength for every challenge.]" John 14:27 AMP

Shift:

"Dear friends, I warn you as "temporary residents and foreigners" to keep away from worldly desires that wage war against your very souls. Be careful to live properly among your unbelieving neighbors." 1 Peter 2:11 NLT

Devotional # 19

Be Present

"For though I am absent from you in body, I am present with you in spirit and delight to see how disciplined you are and how firm your faith in Christ is." Colossians 2:5 NIV

Absent but present. Spirit to Body.

This reminds me of one of the states of matter; Gas. Although it is absent in form, it is very present. And to give gas or air a form in order to become a solid state of matter, we must capture it in a shell or some type of vessel in which it will be able to take the shape, form and appearance of the vessel it occupies.

God is a spirit. Not only so but when Christ arose from the grave to go back to his father, he sent us the Holy Spirit. And that Holy Spirit moves around us freely looking for vessels to reside in. Looking for a heart to dwell in. Looking for a temple (Body, Mind, & Heart).

"Behold, I stand at the door, and knock: if any man hear my voice, and open the door, I will come in to him, and will sup with him, and he with me." Revelation 3:20 KJV

When we make the decision to accept Christ's sacrifice and receive the Holy Spirit, we are no longer our own. Our lives become hid in Christ and we become physical members of Christ himself. He lives. There's an old hymn that says, 'He lives, he lives, Christ Jesus lives today. He walks with me and talks with me, along life's narrow way. He lives, he lives,

Christ Jesus lives today. You ask me how I know he lives, he lives within my heart'.

1 Corinthians 6:19 NIV says "Do you not know that your bodies are temples of the Holy Spirit, who is in you, whom you have received from God? You are not your own;" He lives in each and every one of us who have made the exchange. So our battles are not our own because we are no longer our own. Our battles belong to God who is very present in our lives through the Holy Spirit that lives within us.

And he delights in us so much that he is patient with us because he does not want us to perish (2 Peter 3:9). He makes available every opportunity and lays out a way of escape every time. And when we delight in him, he gives us the desires of our heart (Psalm 37:4).

"Let us consider how to stir up one another to love and good works, not neglecting to meet together, as is the habit of some, but encouraging one another, and all the more as you see the Day drawing near." Hebrews 10:24-25 ESV

Be present in your family. Be present to your friends. Be present in your church. Be present in your neighborhood. Be present in your community. Be Present as he is Present.

19 - Scriptures

Motivate:

"What is the benefit, my fellow believers, if someone claims to have faith but has no [good] works [as evidence]? Can that [kind of] faith save him? [No, a mere claim of faith is not sufficient--genuine faith produces good works.]" James 2:14 AMP

Teach:

"If a brother or sister is without [adequate] clothing and lacks [enough] food for each day, and one of you says to them, "Go in peace [with my blessing], [keep] warm and feed yourselves," but he does not give them the necessities for the body, what good does that do? So too, faith, if it does not have works [to back it up], is by itself dead [inoperative and ineffective]." James 2:15-17 AMP

Win:

"Be kind and helpful to one another, tender-hearted [compassionate, understanding], forgiving one another [readily and freely], just as God in Christ also forgave you." Ephesians 4:32 AMP

Trust:

"Honour thy father and thy mother: and, Thou shalt love thy neighbour as thyself." Matthew 19:19 KJV

Fear-Not:

"And though one can overpower him who is alone, two can resist him. A cord of three strands is not quickly broken." Ecclesiastes 4:12 AMP

Shift: _____

"We [earnestly] urge you, believers, admonish those who are out of line [the undisciplined, the unruly, the disorderly], encourage the timid [who lack spiritual courage], help the [spiritually] weak, be very patient with everyone [always controlling your temper]." 1 Thessalonians 5:14 AMP

Devotional # 20

Remembering Mercies, Humbled in Grace, Elevated through Favor

How many times have you been rejected in your life? Overlooked, Abandoned, lead astray? Sometimes we don't realize how much we've endured and had to go through. Things that we are embarrassed to speak about, and sometimes we just don't even want to think about it. Some people look at us and see such great things and potential. They see where we're going, what we're doing, what we're good/gifted at, when sometimes we ourselves can't help but see where we've been, where we still are.

But if we were to forget our troubles and tribulations, we wouldn't be able to see just how much those events, moments, tragedies, failures, have cost us, shaped us, and how God has brought us out, time after time again. Remembering the Lord's mercies (whether great or small) can help us to remain humble during the journey of where God is taking us.

Some may feel that being humble means that you get overlooked or turned down often, or that it may make you miss out on opportunities or open doors in its season, because you're just not pushy enough or not bold enough to capture the times when it matters. But being humble really has a lot to do with the position that you take when an opportunity has been given by Grace. It comes with a special honor because it leaves much room to move up higher, through favor, in the presence of those around you.

Because you have been through a lot in life, it doesn't just automatically grant you a position of honor. Honor is earned by being willing and humble enough to take the place of the least. In Luke 14:7-11 NIV, at the house of a Pharisee, Jesus [...noticed how the guests picked the places of honor at the table, he told them this parable: "When someone invites you to a wedding feast, do not take the place of honor, for a person more distinguished than you may have been invited. If so, the host who invited both of you will come and say to you, 'Give this person your seat.' Then, humiliated, you will have to take the least important place. But when you are invited, take the lowest place, so that when your host comes, he will say to you, 'Friend, move up to a better place.' Then you will be honored in the presence of all the other guests. For all those who exalt themselves will be humbled, and those who humble themselves will be exalted."]

When we exalt ourselves, we take a boastful approach in our works towards the gift of Grace that God has granted us. This shouldn't be, "For it is by grace you have been saved, through faith—and this is not from yourselves, it is the gift of God—not by works, so that no one can boast. For we are God's handiwork, created in Christ Jesus to do good works, which God prepared in advance for us to do." (Ephesians 2:8-10 NIV).

If God has prepared these good works in advance for us, then he has certainly already prepared the way. Therefore, he knows us. He knows what we are capable of, what we have lost along the way. He knows what we had to give up because of the journey, branches that had to be pruned. Gifts and talents that were buried. Scars that have been opened and closed many times over, forming sores and scabs that we've continuously nursed for years. He knows the pain, the suffering we had to endure, when we are barely hanging on by a thread, when we are in need of a word just in due time, a hug, a smile, a phone call, a song, just a little encouragement or in need of some form of confirmation. He knows when we are broken and need to be put back together. He knows when we have been let down, unsupported, left to fend for ourselves by those whom we held dear. He knows because we are God's handiwork.

But despite what we've been through, there are no esteemed entitlement that places us at the head of a table that we have been invited to as a guest. There are no works that justifies an opportunity instituted by Grace. Even though David was chosen to be King, he still humbled himself and played the harp for King Saul when he was called upon, as that was the opportunity that Grace had provided. We should always be humble enough to be counted with the least. Exalting ourselves is of no reward in the kingdom of God, but if we humble ourselves before the Lord, he will exalt us (James 4:10).

Everything has its place, and even in our humbleness, let us not disregard our tests and our trials because they do matter. As we mature spiritually, God will teach us how to learn from and use our testimonies to encourage and build up the body of Christ, to show his great glory and demonstrate his love towards his children. And each testimony will have its opportunity, in the right environment, to be effective onto righteousness, whether it be for one or many.

Remember the Lord's mercies.

Be humbled in his Grace.

Be elevated through Favor.

20 - Scriptures

Motivate:

"It is of the Lord's mercies that we are not consumed, because his compassions fail not." Lamentations 3:22 KJV.

Teach:

"Likewise, you younger men [of lesser rank and experience], be subject to your elders [seek their counsel]; and all of you, clothe yourselves with humility toward one another [tie on the servant's apron], for God is opposed to the proud [the disdainful, the presumptuous, and He defeats them], but He gives grace to the humble." 1 Peter 5:5 AMP

Win:

"For the Lord takes pleasure in His people; He will beautify the humble with salvation." Psalm 149:4 AMP.

Trust:

"For the Lord God is a sun and shield; the Lord bestows favor and honor. No good thing does he withhold from those who walk uprightly." Psalm 84:11 ESV

Fear-Not:

"For thus says the High and Lofty One Who inhabits eternity, whose name is Holy: "I dwell in the high and holy place, With him who has a contrite and humble spirit, To revive the spirit of the humble, And to revive the heart of the contrite ones." Isaiah 57:15 NKJV.

Shift:

"If my people, which are called by my name, shall humble themselves, and pray, and seek my face, and turn from their wicked ways; then will I hear from heaven, and will forgive their sin, and will heal their land." 2 Chronicles 7:14 KJV.

Devotional # 21

The Manual

"All scripture is given by inspiration of God, and is profitable for doctrine, for reproof, for correction, for instruction in righteousness: That the man of God may be perfect, thoroughly furnished unto all good works." 2 Timothy 3:16-17 KJV

"All Scripture is God-breathed [given by divine inspiration] and is profitable for instruction, for conviction [of sin], for correction [of error and restoration to obedience], for training in righteousness [learning to live in conformity to God's will, both publicly and privately—behaving honorably with personal integrity and moral courage]; so that the man of God may be complete and proficient, outfitted and thoroughly equipped for every good work." 2 Timothy 3:16-17 AMP

I found it necessary to display this verse in two versions. It is always wise to review at least a couple different bible versions when you are expounding on scripture. It adds to understanding as well as opens our minds to the illumination of the Word of God to really grasp the fullness of the scripture.

What the scripture is saying is that there is no experience in life that the bible is not suitable to handle. It equips us with direction, it tells us when we've done the wrong thing, it corrects our wrongdoing and shifts us back to a rightful place. It teaches us how to present ourselves both in our appearance and in our behavior when people can see us as well as keeping us from contradicting ourselves when we think that no one is looking. What a thorough manual the bible is. It covers everything. After all, we are created beings; handcrafted from the greatest mastermind you could ever know. The great 'I am' who does everything well.

An Excel program cannot be used to the full capacity of it's given abilities unless the user has studied it's manual and has become well versed with all of its functions and even then, most of the users knowledge is useless because they are still limited to the functions of the realistic requirements in their current position.

In the same way, we cannot be used of God to the fullest of capacity or even know of all the talents and gifts that he has placed within us and all that we are capable of doing and the bountiful blessings that he has stored up for us, unless we study our manual, the bible, and allow God to direct us into his perfect will, revealing a life that he has planned for us from the beginning. The difference between life and an excel program is that God's plan will bring us through many different stages, encounters and experiences, and positions and seasons, as well as allowing us to repeat them again at different levels of maturity; each moment allowing us to utilize a wide array of our knowledge to become complete and proficient. And all of that is catered and customized to our individual personality, mindset, environment, gifts, and talents.

God's plan for us also includes the desires of our hearts, because it is the dwelling place of the Holy Spirit that moves within us, giving us power and love and self-control, so that we can speak those things into existence, soften even the toughest heart with love, and humble ourselves when we are placed in abundance or authority over many. This helps us to not get high-minded, lackadaisical, and negligent with what God has entrusted us with, forgetting that it is all made possible through the Favor of God.

Just think, that are so many people that God can use, and is currently using, and he chose you. Like Noah, you have found favor in the eyes of the Lord. Don't take for granted the time that you spend with God. Heed to his word and to your calling; Know that "...No good thing will he withhold from them that walk uprightly." Psalm 84:11 KJV

21 - Scriptures

Motivate: _____

"And the Lord will continually guide you, and satisfy your soul in scorched and dry places, and give strength to your bones; and you will be like a watered garden, and like a spring of water whose waters do not fail." Isaiah 58:11 AMP

Teach: _____

"But he answered and said, It is written, Man shall not live by bread alone, but by every word that proceedeth out of the mouth of God." Matthew 4:4 KJV

Win: _____

"Sanctify them through thy truth: thy word is truth." John 17:17 KJV

Trust: _____

"Thy word have I hid in mine heart, that I might not sin against thee." Psalm 119:11 KJV

Fear-Not: _____

"Heaven and earth shall pass away, but my words shall not pass away." Matthew 24:35 KJV

Shift: _____

"But prove yourselves doers of the word [actively and continually obeying God's precepts], and not merely listeners [who hear the word but fail to internalize its meaning], deluding yourselves [by unsound reasoning contrary to the truth]." James 1:22 AMP

Devotional # 22

From One to Many!

It is unrealistic to believe that the sin of one does not affect the many (good and bad alike). But there's hope, the sacrifice of one also affects the many. "Christ was sacrificed once to take away the sins of many; and he will appear a second time, not to bear sin, but to bring salvation to those who are waiting for him." Hebrews 9:28 NIV

22 - Scriptures

Motivate: _____

"But God showed his great love for us by sending Christ to die for us while we were still sinners." Romans 5:8 NLT

Teach: _____

"Do not merely look out for your own personal interests, but also for the interests of others." Philippians 2:4 AMP

Win: _____

"Through Him, therefore, let us at all times offer up to God a sacrifice of praise, which is the fruit of lips that thankfully acknowledge *and* confess *and* glorify His name." Hebrews 13:15 AMP

Trust: _____

"Coming to Him *as to* a living stone, rejected indeed by men, but chosen by God *and* precious, you also, as living stones, are being built up a spiritual house, a holy priesthood, to offer up spiritual sacrifices acceptable to God through Jesus Christ." NKJV

Fear-Not: _____

"And He [that same Jesus] is the propitiation for our sins [the atoning sacrifice that holds back the wrath of God that would otherwise be directed at us because of our sinful nature—our worldliness, our lifestyle]; and not for ours alone, but also for [the sins of all believers throughout] the whole world." 1 John 2:2 AMP

Shift: _____

For the life of the flesh is in the blood, and I have given it to you on the altar to make atonement for your souls; for it is the blood that makes atonement, by reason of the life [which it represents].'
Leviticus 17:11 AMP

Devotional # 23

Be Wary of Being Weary

All the way back to Adam and Eve, sin has caused us to have a laborious life. Back in Genesis, God cursed the ground because of the sin that Adam and Eve committed, and he said to Adam "By the sweat of your brow you will eat your food until you return to the ground, since from it you were taken; for dust you are and to dust you will return." Genesis 3:19 NIV. To Eve he cursed with painful labor in giving birth.

No matter how you look at it, this is our plight, and none is exempt. This laborious curse has further manifested itself in many ways throughout all of the issues of life. Surely life can get wearisome, and you don't have to be tilling the ground to feel that way. Even in the very things in life that we try to do to lift our standard or way of living or to pursue our dreams and passions in life; All of it comes with many labors and when one is weary there's only one viable option; Rest.

Rest is the act of ceasing work or movement. A state of inactivity, minimal function; Sleep. We know the Bible says, "Come to me, all you who are weary and burdened, and I will give you rest. Take my yoke upon you and learn from me, for I am gentle and humble in heart, and you will find rest for your souls." Matthew 11:28-29 NIV. Surely, we can all use some rest from our busy day to day lives; but the rest that Jesus was talking about was not physical rest. God is a Spirit, so we ought to also consider the strain and burdens that the issues of life have put on our spirit man and consequently our souls. Our souls have been working overtime capturing all the weight of our life's story while our spirit have been crying out for us to make the exchange. What is that exchange? It's the exchange of accepting the yoke of Christ, learning from him how to be made free from the wearisome burden of sin that he sacrificed himself for, in order that we can return to relationship with God, the father, just like he did.

Let's read that verse again... "Come to me, all you who are weary and burdened, and I will give you rest. Take my yoke upon you and learn from me, for I am gentle and humble in heart, and you will find rest for your souls." Matthew 11:28-29 NIV.

On the contrary, what does God say about Physical deeds? Galatians 6:9 NIV says "Let us not become weary in doing good, for at the proper time we will reap a harvest if we do not give up."

Be wary of being weary. No productivity comes from the weary. When we are weary, we are more inclined to give up, to miss out, and to lose hope. When you feel taxed, beat up, abused, overused, unappreciated, unnoticed, overlooked, passed over, frustrated, mistreated, forgotten, ignored, drained, exhausted, tired, disliked, despised, overworked, neglected, dismissed, disregarded, rejected, resented, insulted, avoided, undervalued, belittled, discredited, criticized, disrespected, held back, minimized, weakened, depressed, discouraged, saddened, bothered, helpless, hopeless, and so much more; know that Jesus says, Come to me and make the exchange. Give him what you are carrying and take what he has to give you. We may be carrying all those things and more, that has been a heavy load, but Christ is saying take my yoke, "for my yoke is easy and my burden is light." Matthew 11:30 NIV

So do not become weary in doing good, make the exchange and don't give up. The time is coming when you will reap a harvest. A harvest of love, a harvest of blessings, a harvest of favor, whatever it is that you need, whatever you desire, make the exchange and keep going, keep pushing, keep pressing, keep believing, keep hoping, keep giving it over to the Lord.

23 - Scriptures

Motivate: _____

"For it is [not your strength, but it is] God who is effectively at work in you, both to will and to work [that is, strengthening, energizing, and creating in you the longing and the ability to fulfill your purpose] for His good pleasure." Philippians 2:13 AMP

Teach: _____

"In everything I showed you [by example] that by working hard in this way you must help the weak and remember the words of the Lord Jesus, that He Himself said, 'It is more blessed [and brings greater joy] to give than to receive." Acts 20:35 AMP

Win: _____

"I can do all things through Christ which strengtheneth me." Philippians 4:13 KJV

Trust: _____

"Do you not know? Have you not heard? The Everlasting God, the Lord, the Creator of the ends of the earth Does not become tired or grow weary; There is no searching of His understanding." Isaiah 40:28 AMP

Fear-Not: _____

"For I [fully] satisfy the weary soul, and I replenish every languishing *and* sorrowful person." Jeremiah 31:25 AMP

Shift: _____

"But you *are* a chosen generation, a royal priesthood, a holy nation, His own special people, that you may proclaim the praises of Him who called you out of darkness into His marvelous light;" 1 Peter 2:9 NKJV

Devotional # 24

Rainy Outlook

People have mixed feelings about rain. Some depend on it to water their plants, lawn, etc. or to simply cool things down. Others look at the rain as something that is a messy inconvenience. When it's raining you may even hear people make negative remarks about the rainy weather. We also hear it used in association with statements of misfortune, like when it rains on someone's wedding day.

The reality is that rain is not a negative element nor is it a misfortune. Rain is a sign that it is your season for increase, both in the natural and in the Spiritual.

Leviticus 26:4 NIV says that "I will send you rain in its season, and the ground will yield its crops and the trees their fruit." Rain and every form of water from the heavens were created purposefully for the earth and specifically to sustain it.

At first it may seem that rain is dampening; and for sure it is. In order for rain to have its effects there is a saturation period; and that may not feel so nice. If you've ever looked at the soil when it rains or when you water a plant, depending on the density of the soil, it may look like the water is drowning the base of the plant; but that is only temporary. You'd also notice that the bigger, taller, more mature and the more grounded the trees are, is the harder or denser that the ground is, which affects how quickly the water is absorbed. So, it takes the water a bit longer to seep into those grounds. Potted plants that are weaker, smaller, much shorter and way more fragile, you'd notice that within seconds the water is making its way out through the holes in the bottom of the planter or flower pot; because the water flows more freely through less dense soil.

Sometimes we look at our situation and some of the things in our life that we considered great blessings from God, and as the time goes on, eventually it can come to a point where we begin to feel like we're drowning. We try to stand strong, stay alert, pray, but the drowning that seemed to overwhelm us in one main area, so quickly begins its process of affecting every other area of our lives as it reaches our deep roots that sometimes ranges far and wide. This process for us, can seem like forever and makes us realize that there is no place that the water cannot reach.

And guess what? Sometimes as soon as we absorb all that saturation here comes another downpour before we can bearly catch our breath.

My Lord. God has just answered my prayers, blessings are falling. But wait, now it's saturation time again. Can I take this much water? I'm overwhelmed. I'm drowning again. It's affecting everything again. Everyone looks at me like I'm so blessed, so favored. Some even desire to be in my shoes. I can't eat, I can't sleep; The water is up to my neck, but I remain trusting in the Lord because I know that the water will subside.

Finally, it's fully absorbed now. I feel stronger, I can stand up straighter now. I feel renewed. I'm budding, I'm noticing new gifts, new talents, I'm learning new things, I'm building,

I'm spreading my wings. Wow, this feels incredible. Life is really flourishing for me. This is a great season. Look at my seeded fruit that is growing out of me. It makes me proud to say that I am a recipient of God's blessings, of his Grace, of his Mercy, of his Favor. Indeed, I feel like a child of the King.

Then, the ah-ha moment comes. Trees don't eat their own fruit. It is reserved for those who pick the fruit, the Sower and the Eater. Isaiah 55:10 NIV says "As the rain and the snow come down from heaven, and do not return to it without watering the earth and making it bud and flourish, so that it yields seed for the sower and bread for the eater,"

Isaiah 55 continues to say in verse 11-12 NIV, "so is my word that goes out from my mouth: It will not return to me empty, but will accomplish what I desire and achieve the purpose for which I sent it. You will go out in joy and be led forth in peace; the mountains and hills will burst into song before you, and all the trees of the field will clap their hands."

God has sent the rain just as he sent the word from his mouth. It pours out, it saturates, it enriches, it brings increase, and it is fruitful. [God blessed them and said to them, "Be fruitful and increase in number; fill the earth and subdue it."] Genesis 1:28 NIV.

Prepare your soil in anticipation of the rain. You were built to survive the saturation; you were made to flourish.

Is it your season? What's the weather like? What's your rainy outlook?

24 - Scriptures

Motivate: _____

"And the Spirit of God moved upon the face of the waters." Genesis 1:2 KJV

Teach: _____

"And suddenly there came a sound from heaven as of a rushing mighty wind, and it filled all the house where they were sitting." Acts 2:2 KJV

Win: _____

"And there appeared unto them cloven tongues like as of fire, and it sat upon each of them. And they were all filled with the Holy Ghost, …" Acts 2:3-4 KJV

Trust: _____

"For I will pour out water on him who is thirsty, And streams on the dry ground; I will pour out My Spirit on your offspring And My blessing on your descendants;" Isaiah 44:3 AMP

Fear-Not: _____

"When thou passest through the waters, I will be with thee; and through the rivers, they shall not overflow thee …" Isaiah 43:2 KJV

Shift: _____

"Jesus answered, Verily, verily, I say unto thee, Except a man be born of water and of the Spirit, he cannot enter into the kingdom of God." John 3:5 KJV

Devotional #25

The Message – Act 1: The Setup

No matter how many times movies try to have one central message, I always notice that there are several central messages at different sections throughout the movies. Movies are generally made up of a model called a Three-Act Structure. It divides the full story into three parts for the beginning, middle, and end; Some may also call it the Setup, the Confrontation, and the Resolution.

Now, each act not only carries and builds the story, but also conveys a particular message. I've found that if you only look at a portion of a movie, you will never really grasp the conclusive message of that movie, unless it's just too easily predictable. But there are some people who are only really interested in the setup or the beginning act of movies. They just like to see the history behind how things progressed, how the characters grew and honed their skills, the relationships built, and even what mindset the actors were in and the lives that they portrayed before things got crazy and out of control. The good stuff, before things get all haywire, with tons of controversy. In the beginning, mostly allows people to relate to the characters and to dream, and to sometimes put themselves inside the movie, finding their character twin. In the Old Testament, the book of Genesis begins to tell us about the history of God's creation. Genesis 1:1 says that 'In the beginning God created...". Act one, the setup, the beginning. And we can stay in that phase of creation that allows us to continuously dream, and have visions of creating, wanting, having, and seeing things come into fruition. For many of us, it is enough to keep going through life engulfed in the newness of it, the joy and the beauty.

In the New Testament, which is a revealing of the Old Testament, it begins in telling us about the genealogical history of Jesus Christ, how he was conceived, his birth, and him coming into his ministry. Again, act one, the setup, the beginning. And we can stay in that phase of the glory surrounding the star in the east, that led the 3 wise men to Jesus' birthplace. We were drawn to God by music that touched us, the people that lifted us, the preaching that reached places we didn't know it could, and experiences and moments that just drew us to God. There's the awww experience, with the correlation of Jesus being the lamb and born in a stable. All of the joy and seasonal cheer that comes with Christmas, and gifts, and the love that is in the air. Then looking at all the wonderful miracles that Jesus did during his ministry; raising the dead, causing the blind to see, the lame to walk, multiplying resources significantly to feed the multitude. And we can stay in the mindset of what an amazing God we serve that has sent his son that we would have everything we need to continue a meaningful life on this earth.

But then, there is Act 2;

25 - Scriptures

Motivate: _____

"Now the God of hope fill you with all joy and peace in believing, that ye may abound in hope, through the power of the Holy Ghost." Romans 15:13 KJV

Teach: _____

"Thou wilt shew me the path of life: in thy presence is fulness of joy; at thy right hand there are pleasures for evermore." Psalm 16:11 KJV

Win: _____

"But seek ye first the kingdom of God, and his righteousness; and all these things shall be added unto you." Matthew 6:33 KJV

Trust: _____

"Truly the light is sweet, and a pleasant thing it is for the eyes to behold the sun" Ecclesiastes 11:7 KJV

Fear-Not: _____

"For ye shall go out with joy, and be led forth with peace: the mountains and the hills shall break forth before you into singing, and all the trees of the field shall clap their hands." Isaiah 55:12 KJV

Shift: _____

"Until now you have not asked [the Father] for anything in My name; but now ask and keep on asking and you will receive, so that your joy may be full and complete." John 16:24 AMP

Devotional # 26

The Message – Act 2: The Confrontation

Some people gravitate more to the action-packed adventure scenes that give us a jolt and set our hearts racing. The rising action where the stakes get higher. There's more to lose, more to gain, and we're just not sure which way things will turn out. We're at the edge of our seats waiting for the next thing. Wham, bam, it hits us without expectation. It rattles our emotions; shakes our stability. So much is said, so much is happening, the worst possible thing that we could ever imagine is going to happen. We cringe, we look away, we even hold our breath, and sometimes tears begin to form when it's all said and done. Where does this leave everything.

For some, these experiences happen so often that they thrive on living life on the edge. They don't care about the beginning or the end, just throw them into the water and they'll find out if they'll sink or swim. They want the rush of climbing the cliff, walking at the edge of the mountain, running for their lives. They take life's rollercoasters with their hands in air, while other stomachs relocate to their mouths. Some are admitted into the hospital during this phase, just buckling under the stress and pressure. Some are left seeking help, not knowing which way to turn and what decisions to make. Some even turn to drugs and drinking and many addictions as coping mechanisms. Needless to say, some don't just crumble under the unsuspecting weights, but also succumb to the many labels that gets slapped on them, because it comes with the territory.

In Joshua chapter 6, the Lord had torn down the walls of Jericho that encircled the city of possibly 7-9 acres, in great victory. However, even after clear instructions from the Lord to keep themselves from taking anything from the city for personal gain, unbeknownst to Joshua, one man caused their further victories to come to a crashing halt as they went up to the city of Ai to conquer it.

Joshua 7:4-14 AMP says that [... about three thousand men from the sons of Israel went up there, but they fled [in retreat] from the men of Ai. The men of Ai killed about thirty-six of Israel's men, and chased them from the gate as far as [the bluffs of] Shebarim and struck them down as they descended [the steep pass], so the hearts of the people melted [in despair and began to doubt God's promise] and became like water disheartened). Then Joshua tore his clothes and fell face downward on the ground before the ark of the Lord until evening, he and the elders of Israel; and [with great sorrow] they put dust on their heads. Joshua said, "Alas, O Lord God, why have You brought this people across the Jordan at all, only to hand us over to the Amorites, to destroy us? If only we had been willing to live beyond the Jordan! O Lord, what can I say now that [the army of] Israel has turned back [in retreat and fled] before their enemies? For the Canaanites and all the inhabitants of the land will hear about it, and will surround us and cut off our name from the earth. And what will You do for Your great name [to keep it from dishonor]?" So the Lord said to Joshua, "Get up! Why is it that you have fallen on your face? Israel has sinned; they have also transgressed My covenant which I commanded them [to keep]. They have even taken some of the things under the ban, and they have both stolen and denied [the theft]. Moreover, they have also put the stolen objects among their own things. That is why the soldiers of Israel could not stand [and defend themselves] before their enemies; they turned their backs [and ran] before them, because they have become accursed. I will not be with you anymore unless you destroy the things under the ban from among you. Rise up! Consecrate the people and say, 'Consecrate yourselves for tomorrow, for thus says the Lord, the God of Israel: "There are things under the ban among you, O Israel. You cannot stand [victorious] before your enemies until you remove the things under the ban from among you."]

Act 2 the confrontation, are the moments that everyone knows we'll have to face, because we make mistakes, we fall short. There are consequences. There are so many Act twos throughout the bible; Practically in every book. In Luke 22 Jesus was seized and taken away leading up to his crucifixion. In vs. 54-62 AMP Peter had several confrontations during those intense moments where he knew what was going to happen to Jesus and he instinctively, responded trying to save his own life, and found himself in a deeply grieved and distressed place. The scripture says…

"And Peter was following at a [safe] distance. After they had kindled a fire in the middle of the courtyard and had sat down together, Peter sat among them. And a servant-girl, seeing him as he sat in the firelight and looking intently at him, said, "This man was with Him too." But Peter denied it, saying, "Woman, I do not know Him!" A little later someone

else saw him and said, "You are one of them too." But Peter said, "Man, I am not!" After about an hour had passed, another man began to insist, "This man was with Him, for he is a Galilean too." But Peter said, "Man, I do not know what you are talking about." Immediately, while he was still speaking, a rooster crowed. The Lord turned and looked at Peter. And Peter remembered the word of the Lord, how He had told him, "Before a rooster crows today, you will deny Me three times." And he went out and wept bitterly [deeply grieved and distressed]."

These are the moments that we tend to look away and not grasp the message there, because it is too painful, too gruesome, too sacrificial. We'll have to give up too much, loose too much. It's not a nice feeling when we're being chastened, or reprimanded, or when we must fall to our knees and ask for forgiveness or further, come face to face and admit our wrong or deal with the mental anguish of acknowledgement.

The message! What message? We can't see it when we are in a mode of defeat, and when everything that could go wrong, has gone wrong. When we said we wouldn't and we did; When our emotions, shame and embarrassment has taken over; when selfishness, greed, anger, resentment, hurt and pain has come to the forefront of our hearts and minds. What message? We don't want to be there long enough to grasp the intricacies of what led to the moment, because we have so many excuses and so many reasons for why we did what we did.

We may have thought it was our only opportunity, our only chance, our only door, the only way and we couldn't get around it. We may have thought we did what we had to do and given the same circumstances and the same options, if we had another chance to replace our steps, we might possibly end up doing the same thing over again. At this point, some of our reasoning skills and ability to understand, including lack of wisdom, struggle to block us out of the next phase; Act 3.

26 - Scriptures

Motivate: _____

"In every situation [no matter what the circumstances] be thankful *and* continually give thanks *to God*; for this is the will of God for you in Christ Jesus." 1 Thessalonians 5:18 AMP

Teach: _____

"For God speaks once, and even twice, yet no one notices it…" Job 33:14 AMP

Win: _____

"In a dream, a vision of the night [one may hear God's voice], When deep sleep falls on men While slumbering upon the bed, Then He opens the ears of men and seals their instruction, That He may turn man aside *from his* conduct, And keep him from pride;" Job 33:15-17 AMP

Trust: _____

"For I reckon that the sufferings of this present time are not worthy to be compared with the glory which shall be revealed in us." Romans 8:18 KJV

Fear-Not: _____

"Fear thou not; for I am with thee: be not dismayed; for I am thy God: I will strengthen thee; yea, I will help thee; yea, I will uphold thee with the right hand of my righteousness." Isaiah 41:10 KJV

Shift: _____

"For our momentary, light distress [this passing trouble] is producing for us an eternal weight of glory [a fullness] beyond all measure [surpassing all comparisons, a transcendent splendor and an endless blessedness]!" 2 Corinthians 4:17 AMP

Devotional # 27

The Message – Act 3: The Resolution

At this point some people's nerves are still too wired to simmer down and relax into the resolved state of the final message (The reason that the beginning began, in the first place).

At the end of the Three-Act Structure, the final section, Act Three - The Resolution, things come to a wrap-up. Lives are altered and changed. Lessons are learned and clarified. New paths are made, new ways discovered. Confrontations end up being concerted; coordinated into their rightful place of importance, or united into a mending effort of new bonds and refreshed re-fired relationships.

A lot of people live for the ending of movies and stories. And sometimes getting to the ending takes a very long time, that many don't have the patience for. But Romans 5:3 AMP says "hardship (distress, pressure, trouble) produces patient endurance" [*See Devotional #52 'Perfecting Patience*].

There may even be some that want to skip straight to the end. But endings are not always what we expect them to be. In this cycle of life, one end is always a new beginning. Even in movies these days, everyone stays put at the end of the movie watching the writings and credits scroll up on the wall just to see if there is a glimpse of another movie to come, birthed out of the ending of the current one. But one thing is for sure, all the messages of the beginning, middle and end collectively create something whole.

Have you ever baked a pizza? There is a Three-Act Structure of preparing a pizza (Purchase the supplies, knead the dough, and lay the toppings. That end becomes a new beginning, then you have another Three-Act Structure of Baking, cutting and eating. In both examples the easiest parts are act 1, purchasing and baking. The Act 2's are purposeful confrontations of kneading and cutting. When we knead the dough, it goes through combining active ingredients, stretching, rolling, and even pressing. And cutting, slices right through everything that connected the whole pie together, not even considering that some of the toppings that were laid precisely will also be severed. But Act 3 allows us to savor a moment of reflection of all the toppings that have been laid and layered, whether sparingly or generously, and the savoring of the taste of all of that, surely brings it to a final resolution, a close, one central message or in this case flavor or taste.

Our resolution is Our Revelation.

Revelation 1:8 ESV says "I am the Alpha and the Omega," says the Lord God, "who **is** and who **was** and who **is to come**, the Almighty."

27 - Scriptures

Motivate:

"Then God spoke all these words: I am the Lord your God, who has brought you out of the land of Egypt, out of the house of slavery. "You shall have no other gods before Me. "You shall not make for yourself any idol, or any likeness (form, manifestation) of what is in heaven above or on the earth beneath or in the water under the earth [as an object to worship]. You shall not worship them nor serve them; for I, the Lord your God, am a jealous (impassioned) God …" Exodus 20:1-4 AMP

Teach:

"I am Alpha and Omega, the beginning and the end, the first and the last." Revelation 22:13 KJV

Win:

"And Zacchaeus stood and said to the Lord, "Behold, Lord, the half of my goods I give to the poor. And if I have defrauded anyone of anything, I restore it fourfold." And Jesus said to him, "Today salvation has come to this house, since he also is a son of Abraham. For the Son of Man came to seek and to save the lost." Luke 19:8-10 ESV

Trust:

"Jesus looked up and saw the rich putting their gifts into the offering box, and he saw a poor widow put in two small copper coins. And he said, "Truly, I tell you, this poor widow has put in more than all of them. For they all contributed out of their abundance, but she out of her poverty put in all she had to live on." Luke 21:1-4 ESV

Fear-Not: _____

"Then Jesus said to him, "Put your sword back in its place; for all those who *habitually* draw the sword will die by the sword. Do you think that I cannot appeal to My Father, and He will immediately provide Me with more than twelve legions of angels? How then will the Scriptures be fulfilled, that it must happen this way?" Matthew 26:52-54 AMP

Shift: _____

"But the Helper (Comforter, Advocate, Intercessor—Counselor, Strengthener, Standby), the Holy Spirit, whom the Father will send in My name [in My place, to represent Me and act on My behalf], He will teach you all things. And He will help you remember everything that I have told you." John 14:26 AMP

Devotional # 28

Concerning Prayer

Prayer is something that many people have different opinions about. Some gravitate towards it and others don't. Some value it as an essential part of their daily life and others, only when they feel the need to. One opinion is the notion, that one has to know How to pray in order To pray. And another, is that one has to be righteous in order for God to hear them and answer.

One thing for sure is that Prayer is purposeful. In fact, it is a Purposeful Talk with God. There is no right place or wrong place to talk to God. There isn't a right mood or a wrong mood to be in, in order to communicate with God. There isn't a right position or a wrong position to get into, in order to speak to God. We can speak to him in our minds, out loud, by ourselves, or in a group. We can speak to him on our knees, lying down, driving, cooking, eating, in the bath/shower, running, walking, standing or sitting. We can talk to him with our eyes closed or open, while we're upset, annoyed, frustrated, sad, or happy; while we're bursting with excitement, or hopeful with expectation or just at peace and waiting.

Philippians 4:6 NKJV says " ...in everything by prayer and supplication, with thanksgiving, let your requests be made known to God". In everything. While prayer can shift between the act of making a request, and the expression of thanksgiving or worship; Supplication guides us into prayer requests by indicating how we should come to God to present, state, ask, or petition for our request; Which is, by humbling ourselves and displaying thankfulness because of our confidence in God, knowing that he is able to do exceedingly abundantly above all that we can ask or think.

Last but not least (in fact, this really should be first). One of the most important aspects of prayer is cleansing and forgiveness. Proverbs 28:13 ESV says "Whoever conceals his transgressions will not prosper, but he who confesses and forsakes them will obtain mercy."

One of the reasons why many people say that their prayers go unanswered, unheard, or is ineffective, is because of blockages. Isaiah 59:1-3 ESV says, "Behold, the Lord's hand is not shortened, that it cannot save, or his ear dull, that it cannot hear; but your iniquities have made a separation between you and your God, and your sins have hidden his face from you so that he does not hear." When we come to God and humble ourselves, it requires the action of consistently (each time we come to him with a request) asking for cleansing and forgiveness for anything we have said, done, or thought (both consciously and unconsciously), that was wrong or goes against the will of God for our lives. And it is important that we make this personal.

Why? Because many times there are things that we have done wrong that may not necessarily be considered wrong for others based on God's will for their lives. James 4:17 ESV says "So whoever knows the right thing to do and fails to do it, **for him it is sin**." We shouldn't only consider as sin, those times when we may have behaved with outright disrespect, foul-mouth, and inexcusable behaviors and attitudes. But what about our lack of obedience when God has given us direction and we decided to do things our way; Times when he gave us a way out or a way in, and we talked ourselves into a hundred reasons why we shouldn't or why it's not the right time for us; And times when we've allowed distraction, blindness, and immaturity to cloud our judgement.

Let's be real, some things are unavoidable based on our lack of wisdom, experience, and judgement (the definition of naive); as well as our lack of understanding. This is why, the bible has already acknowledged that none are without sin. Ecclesiastes 7:20 ESV says "Surely there is not a righteous man on earth who does good and never sins." Moses, David, Paul, etc., they were not without sin. When we're pushed to the max, overexposed to negativity, overglazed with desire, or overly laid back and slack, we can easily fall out of the will of God, consciously, unconsciously, and willfully. But we have a responsibility to bring ourselves before the Lord and confess earnestly and to make amends.

Jesus is our advocate, but he will not confess nor make amends for us. Some people may think that when one makes amends, we smooth and cover over and make up for what we did wrong. But if we only put our sin on the bench for when our positively good key players get hurt, then the sin gets right back in the game again. The definition of making amends is to change, modify for the better, or alter to correct the error. Without the change of mind and heart to destroy, discard, and move forward on a better note, then our confession is useless.

28 - Scriptures

Motivate:

"With all prayer and petition pray [with specific requests] at all times [on every occasion and in every season] in the Spirit, and with this in view, stay alert with all perseverance and petition [interceding in prayer] for all God's people." Ephesians 6:18 AMP

Teach:

"But when you pray, go into your most private room, close the door and pray to your Father who is in secret, and your Father who sees [what is done] in secret will reward you." Matthew 6:6 AMP

Win:

"In the same way the Spirit [comes to us and] helps us in our weakness. We do not know what prayer to offer or how to offer it as we should, but the Spirit Himself [knows our need and at the right time] intercedes on our behalf with sighs and groanings too deep for words." Romans 8:26 AMP

Trust:

"After this manner therefore pray ye: Our Father which art in heaven, Hallowed be thy name. Thy kingdom come, Thy will be done in earth, as it is in heaven. ..." Matthew 6:9-10 KJV

Fear-Not:

"Don't worry about anything; instead, pray about everything. Tell God what you need, and thank him for all he has done." Philippians 4:6 NLT

Shift: _____

"Keep actively watching and praying that you may not come into temptation; the spirit is willing, but the body is weak." Matthew 26:41 AMP

Devotional # 29

Freedom of Choice & the effect on prayer

What if we choose to remain in sin due to our rebellious nature, or we're not ready, or we can't immediately change our situation (for whatever the reason), does that prevent us from praying?

Absolutely not. Philippians 2:13 AMP says, "For it is [not your strength, but it is] God who is effectively at work in you, both to will and to work [that is, strengthening, energizing, and **creating in you the longing and the ability to fulfill your purpose**] for His good pleasure.". Romans 8:26-28 AMP says "In the same way the Spirit [comes to us and] helps us in our weakness. We do not know what prayer to offer or how to offer it as we should, but the Spirit Himself [knows our need and at the right time] intercedes on our behalf with sighs and groanings too deep for words. And He who searches the hearts knows what the mind of the Spirit is, because the Spirit intercedes [before God] on behalf of God's people in accordance with God's will. And we know [with great confidence] that God [who is deeply concerned about us] causes all things to work together [as a plan] for good for those who love God, to those who are called according to His plan and purpose."

Romans 12:3 AMP says that "...God has apportioned to each a degree of faith [and a purpose designed for service]." And Romans 10:17 AMP says "...faith comes from hearing [what is told], and what is heard comes by the [preaching of the] message concerning Christ."

So as long as we believe in the Lord and make ourselves available to the word of God, the conviction of the Holy Spirit will work **accordingly and timely** in each of us. 2 Peter 3:9 AMP assures us that even though we don't see certain things happening in our lives because of our sin and disobedience, the Lord is patient. The scripture says that "The Lord does not delay [as though He were unable to act] and is not slow about His promise, as some count slowness, but is [extraordinarily] patient toward you, not wishing for any to perish but for all to come to repentance."

Nevertheless, let us not forget this very important fact. 2 Peter 3:10 tells us that the Lord will come when we least expect it. Verse 14-15 AMP says "since you are looking forward to these things, **be diligent and make every effort to be found by Him** [at His return] spotless and blameless, in peace [that is, inwardly calm with a sense of spiritual well-being and confidence, having lived a life of obedience to Him]. And consider the patience of our Lord [His delay in judging and avenging wrongs] as salvation [that is, allowing time for more to be saved];"

29 - Scriptures

Motivate: _____

"I urge you, first of all, to pray for all people. Ask God to help them; intercede on their behalf, and give thanks for them. Pray this way for kings and all who are in authority so that we can live peaceful and quiet lives marked by godliness and dignity. This is good and pleases God our Savior, who wants everyone to be saved and to understand the truth." 1 Timothy 2:1-4 NLT

Teach: _____

"For there is [only] one God, and [only] one Mediator between God and mankind, the Man Christ Jesus," 1 Timothy 2:5 AMP

Win: _____

"It was for this freedom that Christ set us free [completely liberating us]; therefore keep standing firm and do not be subject again to a yoke of slavery [which you once removed]." Galatians 5:1 AMP

Trust: _____

"If the Son therefore shall make you free, ye shall be free indeed." John 8:36 KJV

Fear-Not: _____

"Now the Lord is the Spirit, and where the Spirit of the Lord is, there is liberty [emancipation from bondage, true freedom]." 2 Corinthians 3:17 AMP

Shift: _____

"Everything is permissible for me, but not all things are beneficial. Everything is permissible for me, but I will not be enslaved by anything [and brought under its power, allowing it to control me]." 1 Corinthians 6:12 AMP

Devotional # 30

All you need is one!

"*There is* one body and one Spirit, just as you were called in one hope of your calling; one Lord, one faith, one baptism; one God and Father of all, who *is* above all, and through all, and in you all." Ephesians 4:4-6 NKJV

There is one, all you need is one, and it only takes one.

It only takes one, to make or break things. One storm, one drunk driver, one volcano, one tornado, one earthquake, one irrational thinker, one who has a deranged mind, or one who only acts based on instinct and no reasoning whatsoever, to destroy everything in one's path, and everything that one has worked hard to build, grow, and pour their everything into.

But it also takes one to restore, one to repay, one to save. John 3:16 KJV says "For God so loved the world, that he gave his **only** begotten Son, ...". And the beauty of the son, Jesus Christ, is what his one body represents. 1 Corinthians 12:12 ESV says "For just as the body is one and has many members, and all the members of the body, though many, are one body, so it is with Christ." That sacrifice of Christ's one body, made the Holy Spirit accessible to all bodies, and gave us a direct connection to God the Father.

John 10:27-30 KJV says that "My sheep hear my voice, and I know them, and they follow me: and I give unto them eternal life, and they shall never perish, neither shall any man pluck them out of my hand. My Father, which gave them to me, is greater than all; and no man is able to pluck them out of my Father's hand. I and my Father are One."

The voice of God is a remarkable voice of purpose that calls us into a oneness in his Kingdom, as we listen to and follow his voice. A voice that takes the time to talk to us because he knows us completely and he knows everything that we are capable of.

And just by simply listening and believing in Christ, he has given us all the benefits of the multitude found in the one body, to do even more than he had the time and the chance to do while he walked this earth (and just in that short time, even that was a lot). John 14:12 ESV says "Truly, truly, I say to you, whoever believes in me will also do the works that I do; and greater works than these will he do, because I am going to the Father."

No matter what your trials and hardships are in life, if you do it alone, you are only one (singular), but if you do it with our one Lord and Savior Jesus Christ, the value of your one (singular) has just been enormously increased (as a plural) and continues to grow with each believer added daily to the one body of Christ. What an enormous return on one investment! The greatest investment you'll ever make that not only has the greatest return on earth but also the greatest reward in heaven.

Today and every day; All you need is one!

30 - Scriptures

Motivate: _____

"Hear, O Israel: The Lord our God is one Lord:" Deuteronomy 6:4 KJV

Teach: _____

"There is one body [of believers] and one Spirit—just as you were called to one hope when called [to salvation]— one Lord, one faith, one baptism, one God and Father of us all who is [sovereign] over all and [working] through all and [living] in all." Ephesians 4:4-6 AMP

Win: _____

"I, even I, am the Lord; and beside me there is no savior." Isaiah 43:11 KJV

Trust: _____

"You believe that God is one; you do well [to believe that]. The demons also believe [that], and shudder and bristle [in awe-filled terror—they have seen His wrath]!" James 2:19 AMP

Fear-Not: _____

"For certain individuals whose condemnation was written about long ago have secretly slipped in among you. They are ungodly people, who pervert the grace of our God into a license for immorality and deny Jesus Christ our only Sovereign and Lord." Jude 1:4 NIV

Shift: _____

"Be sober [well balanced and self-disciplined], be alert and cautious at all times. That enemy of yours, the devil, prowls around like a roaring lion [fiercely hungry], seeking someone to devour." 1 Peter 5:8 AMP

Devotional # 31

Best Self!

Do you ever feel like you're holding back the best of yourself, waiting on that moment to happen where you feel like it's worth the best you? Maybe it's because you don't value the people around you enough to feel like they deserve that extent of you. Or maybe you feel like you'll get hurt, or that you'll end up regretting it later.

What about the feeling like you're being held back from your best self, because it always seems like you're being misjudged? Maybe people feel like you're always trying too hard, or that you're always trying to outdo others even when there's no real reward. So in response, you end up scaling back and treading lightly, not trying as hard and always being self-conscious about keeping yourself from standing out too much. You undervalue your work, and you under-sell yourself, just so that you don't appear beyond people's expectations; maybe so that no one will use you and abuse you. You may even hide your abilities so that you won't have to do anything more than what you already have to do or are required to do...

Colossians 3:23-24 AMP says "Whatever you do [whatever your task may be], work from the soul [that is, put in your very best effort], as [something done] for the Lord and not for men, knowing [with all certainty] that it is from the Lord [not from men] that you will receive the inheritance which is your [greatest] reward. It is the Lord Christ whom you [actually] serve."

Ecclesiastes 9:10 NET says, "Whatever you find to do with your hands, do it with all your might, because there is neither work nor planning nor knowledge nor wisdom in the grave, the place where you will eventually go." Isn't that the truth. The bible says that "... it is appointed and destined for all men to die once and after this [comes certain] judgment," (Hebrews 9:27 AMP). None of us have immortal bodies. Our minds, eyes, feet, you name it, becomes less and less sharp and more and more weak. The different members of our bodies become deteriorated little by little as we inch towards our older ages.

Ecclesiastes 12:1-6 AMP says "Remember [thoughtfully] also your Creator in the days of your youth [for you are not your own, but His], before the evil days come or the years draw near when you will say [of physical pleasures], "I have no enjoyment and delight in them"; before the sun and the light, and the moon and the stars are darkened [by impaired vision], and the clouds [of depression] return after the rain [of tears]; in the day when the keepers of the house (hands, arms) tremble, and the strong men (feet, knees) bow themselves, and the grinders (molar teeth) cease because they are few, and those (eyes) who look through the windows grow dim; when the doors (lips) are shut in the streets and the sound of the grinding [of the teeth] is low, and one rises at the sound of a bird and the crowing of a rooster, and all the daughters of music (voice, ears) sing softly. Furthermore, they are afraid of a high place and of dangers on the road; the almond tree (hair) blossoms [white], and the grasshopper (a little thing) is a burden, and the caperberry (desire, appetite) fails. For man goes to his eternal home and the mourners go about the streets and market places. Earnestly remember your Creator before the silver cord [of life] is broken,..."

While we are living this life, and as we grow in age and maturity; Seriously, thoughtfully, and sincerely consider the Lord and "... whether you eat or drink, or whatever you do, do all to the glory of God." (1 Corinthians 10:31 ESV). We only have one chance to give it our best shot, to do our best work, and to be our best self. And while we speak and communicate with others, let us do so wisely. The things that we say and our communication with others either exposes our best self or our worst self. It exposes our maturity or our immaturity. It lets others know if we are FOR them or against them; or whether we are well informed or lacking information. It promotes us or cancels us out, it compliments or discredits us.

No matter what mistakes we make and how many times we have to correct it and start over or push ourselves to shake it off and move on, our best self is what God desires of us. So don't be afraid to delight yourself in the Lord, because whatever we delight ourselves in, or take joy, pleasure and gladness in, we will give our best selves to. And if we are our best for the Glory of the Lord, then we are our best for the benefit of the Kingdom, we are our best for the benefit of the church, we are our best for the benefit of our members (our bodies), we are our best for the benefit of our family, we are our best for the benefit of our friends, but most of all we are our best for the benefit of ourselves. Yes ourselves. Romans 14:12 ESV says that "... each of us will give an account of himself to God".

So don't let anyone lead you astray by making you feel like you're selfish for seeking after the benefit of salvation for yourself. We can preach and teach and share and encourage and uplift others with the Gospel of Christ, but at the end of the day we still have a responsibility to engage ourselves. We owe it to ourselves to be our best, so that we can inherit the reward of our salvation. In 2 Peter 1, Peter tells us how to make sure that we really are among those that God has called and chosen. He first tells us what we need to do within ourselves in order to be productive and useful and to fall in line with the promises of God, before we can then reveal love and affection to others. Verse 5-6 NLT says to "... Supplement your faith with a generous provision of moral excellence, and moral excellence with knowledge, and knowledge with self-control, and self-control with patient endurance, and patient endurance with godliness," Then Peter says in verse 7 to use that gain of godliness "with brotherly affection, and brotherly affection with love for everyone."

Our best selves are a work in progress and a never ending project, but still it is something to be proud of in every level and at every stage. We will always find memories and moments that could have been better and that we could have done better, but life is not over yet. Our best selves are being perfected (matured) day by day. Reach into your heart and pull out what you have been hiding, what you have been holding back, what you have been pondering upon. It is time to step out into your best you and be your best self.

31 - Scriptures

Motivate: _____

"Whatever you do [whatever your task may be], work from the soul [that is, put in your very best effort], as [something done] for the Lord and not for men," Colossians 3:23 AMP

Teach: _____

"Study and do your best to present yourself to God approved, a workman [tested by trial] who has no reason to be ashamed, accurately handling and skillfully teaching the word of truth." 2 Timothy 2:15 AMP

Win: _____

"In everything I showed you [by example] that by working hard in this way you must help the weak and remember the words of the Lord Jesus, that He Himself said, 'It is more blessed [and brings greater joy] to give than to receive." Acts 20:35 AMP

Trust: _____

"The soul (appetite) of the lazy person craves and gets nothing [for lethargy overcomes ambition], But the soul (appetite) of the diligent [who works willingly] is rich and abundantly supplied." Proverbs 13:4 AMP

Fear-Not: _____

"So, my dear brothers and sisters, be strong and immovable. Always work enthusiastically for the Lord, for you know that nothing you do for the Lord is ever useless." 1 Corinthians 15:58 NLT

Shift: _____

"In all labor there is profit, But mere talk leads only to poverty."
Proverbs 14:23 AMP

Talk of the Tongue
Part II
Devotional #'s 32-43

"Now if we put bits into the horses' mouths to make them obey us, we guide their whole body as well." ...

"In the same sense, the tongue is a small part of the body, and yet it boasts of great things..."
James 3:3 & 5 AMP

Devotional # 32

Who Do Men Say I Am?

"When Jesus came into the region of Caesarea Philippi, He asked His disciples, saying, "Who do men say that I, the Son of Man, am?" So they said, "Some say John the Baptist, some Elijah, and others Jeremiah or one of the prophets." He said to them, "But who do you say that I am?" Simon Peter answered and said, "You are the Christ, the Son of the living God." Jesus answered and said to him, "Blessed are you, Simon Bar-Jonah, for flesh and blood has not revealed this to you, but My Father who is in heaven." Matthew 16:13-17 NKJV

Who do men say that you are? Some may identify who you are by the type of experience that they have personally had with you. Some may identify you by the type of person that they have heard about you, on numerous occasions or by the multitude. Some may Identify you by who you appear to be, or who you show yourself to be. Some may say that you are this and that you are that. Have you asked yourself that question?

Jesus asked the question, earnestly, "Who do men say that I, the Son of Man, am?" He didn't ask that question to the Pharisees and the Sadducees, whom he had just spoken to in the region prior. He asked that question to his beloved disciples. Those who followed him faithfully, who depended on his word, the ones whom he broke down parables to, broke bread with, built a relationship with; the ones to whom he revealed who he truly was. He asked this question to the next generation who he found worthy to bestow the power of the Holy Spirit to be his witnesses, his offspring throughout the earth. And the disciples responded.

They said that some say Jesus is John the Baptist *(the Preacher who baptized and proclaimed about the coming of Christ, preparing the way of the Lord). Luke 3:15-16 NKJV says, [Now as the people were in expectation, and all reasoned in their hearts about John, whether he was the Christ or not, John answered, saying to all, "I indeed baptize you with water; but One mightier than I is coming, whose sandal strap I am not worthy to loose. He will baptize you with the Holy Spirit and fire.]*

They said that some say Jesus is Elijah. *Elijah was a prophet zealous after the Lord. During the reign of King Ahab (who "did evil in the sight of the Lord, more than all who were before him... and did more to provoke the Lord God of Israel to anger than all the kings of Israel who were before him." 1 Kings 16:30 & 33 NKJV), Elijah commanded that there will be no rain for years until he gave the word that the rain will return "and it happened after a while that the brook dried up, because there had been no rain in the land." 1 Kings 17:7 NKJV. During the drought he dared to ask the question to all the people, ["How long will you falter between two opinions? If the Lord is God, follow Him; but if Baal, follow him." But the people answered him not a word.] 1 Kings 18:21 NKJV. [And it came to pass, at the time of the offering of the evening sacrifice, that Elijah the prophet came near and said, "Lord God of Abraham, Isaac, and Israel, let it be known this day that You are God in Israel and I am Your servant, and that I have done all these things at Your word. Hear me, O Lord, hear me, that this people may know that You are the Lord God, and that You have turned their* hearts back to You again." Then the fire of the Lord fell and consumed the burnt sacrifice, and the wood and the stones and the dust, and it licked up the water that was in the trench. Now when all the people saw it, they fell on their faces; and they said, "The Lord, He is God! The Lord, He is God!"] 1 Kings 18:36-38 NKJV [Then Elijah said to Ahab, "Go up, eat and drink; for there is the sound of abundance of rain."...Now it happened in the meantime that the sky became black with clouds and wind, and there was a heavy rain.] 1 Kings 18:44 & 45 NKJV. Elijah was more than a prophet, he was a true servant of God that did not falter but did mighty works by the word of the Lord. And he wasn't just any prophet; he was the last prophet to prepare the way for the Lord, the messenger. The last prophet? Yes. The last prophet sent to prepare the way for Jesus.

[Then Elijah said to the people, "I alone am left a prophet of the Lord; ..."] 1 Kings 18:22 NKJV. Here Elijah was not speaking of his present time, that he was the last prophet in his day, but rather he was foretelling of the future, as the Lord revealed to him. [But the angel said to him, "Do not be afraid, Zacharias, for your prayer is heard; and your wife Elizabeth will bear you a son, and you shall call his name John. And you will have joy and gladness, and many will rejoice at his birth. For he will be great in the sight of the Lord, and shall drink neither wine nor strong drink. He will also be filled with the Holy Spirit, even from his mother's womb. And he will turn many of the children of Israel to the Lord their God. **He will also go before Him in the spirit and power of Elijah**, 'to turn the hearts of the fathers to the children,' and the disobedient to the wisdom of the just, to make ready a people prepared for the Lord."] Luke 1:13-17 NKJV.

In the book of Mark, Jesus spoke to the crowds saying "But what did you [really] go out to see? A prophet? Yes, I tell you, and one [more eminent, more remarkable, and] far more than a prophet [who foretells the future]. This is the one of whom it is written [by the prophet Malachi], 'Behold, I send My messenger ahead of You, Who will prepare Your way before You.' I assure you and most solemnly say to you, among those born of women there has not risen anyone greater than John the Baptist; yet the one who is least in the kingdom of heaven is greater [in privilege] than he. From the days of John the Baptist until now the kingdom of heaven suffers violent assault, and violent men seize it by force [as a precious prize]. For all the prophets and the Law prophesied up until John. And if you are willing to accept it, **John himself is [the fulfillment of] Elijah [as the messenger] who was to come [before the kingdom].*** *" Matthew 11:9-14 AMP.*

You can see why, some men said Jesus was John the Baptist, Elijah, Jeremiah *(the weeping prophet, who was sent to speak to the people that Thus says the Lord; and whose journey can be summed up with these scriptures in an era where the people heard the word but were rebellious and did not take heed)* Jeremiah 6:16-17 AMP says [Thus says the Lord, "Stand by the roads and look; ask for the ancient paths, Where the good way is; then walk in it, And you will find rest for your souls. But they said, 'We will not walk in it!' "I have set watchmen (prophets) over you, Saying, 'Listen and pay attention to the [warning] sound of the trumpet!' But they said, 'We will not listen.'']. Jeremiah 6:27 AMP says ["I [the Lord] have set you as an assayer [O Jeremiah] and as a tester [of the ore] of My people, That you may know and analyze their acts."]

Who do people say you are? Who do they compare you to? They compared Christ to the prophets who spoke the word of the Lord and did the work of God who sent them to prepare the way.

But then Jesus asked the question *"But who do you say that I am?" Simon Peter answered and said, "You are the Christ, the Son of the living God." Matthew 16:15-16 NKJV.* Who does your closely knit circle say you are? Your friends, your family, those who depend on your word, your ways, the things that you say, the things you do, how you do it, those who watch you closely, those whom you influence? Who do they say you are? Would they say that you are walking in the life of whom you were created to be in Christ?

Christ has, is, and forever will be, walking in his calling as the Son of the living God. *"I am He who lives, and was dead, and behold, I am alive forevermore. Amen. And I have the keys of Hades and of Death." Revelation 1:18 NKJV.* Christ has the keys to death. But we have keys too. Through the power of his Holy Spirit, he *says "on this rock I will build My church; and the gates of Hades (death) will not overpower it [by preventing the resurrection of the Christ]. I will give you the keys (authority) of the kingdom of heaven; and whatever you bind [forbid, declare to be improper and unlawful] on earth will have [already] been bound in heaven, and whatever you loose [permit, declare lawful] on earth will have [already] been loosed in heaven." Matthew 16:18-19 AMP.* Amen.

32 - Scriptures

Motivate: _____

"But you are a chosen race, a royal priesthood, a consecrated nation, a [special] people for *God's* own possession, so that you may proclaim the excellencies [the wonderful deeds and virtues and perfections] of Him who called you out of darkness into His marvelous light." 1 Peter 2:9 AMP

Teach: _____

"For we are His workmanship [His own master work, a work of art], created in Christ Jesus [reborn from above—spiritually transformed, renewed, ready to be used] for good works, which God prepared [for us] beforehand [taking paths which He set], so that we would walk in them [living the good life which He prearranged and made ready for us]." Ephesians 2:10 AMP

Win: _____

"Do you not know and understand that you [the church] are the temple of God, and that the Spirit of God dwells [permanently] in you [collectively and individually]?" 1 Corinthians 3:16 AMP

Trust: _____

"You are the salt of the earth; but if the salt has lost its taste (purpose), how can it be made salty? It is no longer good for anything, but to be thrown out and walked on by people" Matthew 5:13 AMP

Fear-Not: _____

"You are the light of [Christ to] the world. A city set on a hill cannot be hidden; nor does *anyone* light a lamp and put it under a basket, but on a lampstand, and it gives light to all who are in the house. Let your light shine before men in such a way that they may see your good deeds *and* moral excellence, and [recognize and honor and] glorify your Father who is in heaven." Matthew 5:14-16 AMP

Shift: _____

"Therefore if anyone is in Christ [that is, grafted in, joined to Him by faith in Him as Savior], he is a new creature [reborn and renewed by the Holy Spirit]; the old things [the previous moral and spiritual condition] have passed away. Behold, new things have come [because spiritual awakening brings a new life]." 2 Corinthians 5:17 AMP

Devotional # 33

Just a Little While Longer

"Humble yourselves therefore under the mighty hand of God, that he may exalt you in due time: Casting all your care upon him; for he careth for you." 1 Peter 5:6-7 KJV

It is important to know when to hold your peace, and when to speak freely. There are so many ways we can communicate, and many of those ways can test our ability to be humble. Many may find it challenging to grasp how to be bold and courageous while still remaining humble. One of the ways to know that you're on the right track, is recognizing that there is a struggle leading up to that point. A struggle between knowing what should or what has to be done, and the sacrifice you have to make in order for the possibility of that change to come. But, once you have made up in your mind to move forward, despite the weight of the task and the risks involved; direction on how, when, and where, will come from God.

One thing that God is a master of, is direction. Isaiah 46:9-10 AMP says [For I am God, and there is no one else; I am God, and there is no one like Me, Declaring the end and the result from the beginning, And from ancient times the things which have not [yet] been done, Saying, 'My purpose will be established, And I will do all that pleases Me and fulfills My purpose,']. John 10:27-30 AMP says "The sheep that are My own hear My voice and listen to Me; I know them, and they follow Me. And I give them eternal life, and they will never, ever [by any means] perish; and no one will ever snatch them out of My hand. My Father, who has given them to Me, is greater and mightier than all; and no one is able to snatch them out of the Father's hand. I and the Father are One [in essence and nature]."

The hand of God is so mighty that Jesus has assured us that because he and the Father are one, there is no fear in moving forward in his direction because we have a two-fold hand of protection, and no one will ever, and no one is able to snatch us out of the mighty hand of God. So, when we humble ourselves under the mighty hand of God, his plan and his purpose will be fulfilled through us. Jeremiah 29:11 AMP says, "For I know the plans and thoughts that I have for you,' says the Lord, 'plans for peace and well-being and not for disaster, to give you a future and a hope." God has already done the great, the magnificent, the powerful, he has created the world and set everything in its cycle, he has done it all. So, what pleases him **and** fulfills his purpose, is to give us a future **and** a hope, and through his plans for us, we will be exalted in due time.

In due time, means an appointed time, a dated time, an ordered time. God who has declared the end and the result from the beginning and have declared in past times the things that is yet to come, He is a master of time. And **he is saying**, don't give up, just a little while longer. And while you wait, **he says** to 'cast your cares upon him, for he cares for you'. You may be experiencing loneliness, opposition, frustrations, but **God says** to cast those worries and those feelings upon him. Communicate with him. Many of us thinks because he sees all and knows all that we don't have to tell him anything. But the bible says, in 2 Chronicles 16:9 AMP " the eyes of the Lord move to and fro throughout the earth so that He may support those whose heart is completely His" **He is looking for you to talk to him**.

Sometimes we make prayer so formal, that some of us make excuses that we don't know how to pray. But the truth is, if we can communicate with others, we can communicate with God. We can also confess our worries and speak to him about our fears, within the confines of our minds and our hearts, so that the enemy cannot use our words against us. We can speak those things which we want in life, out of our mouths so that we can allow it the ability to manifest into the natural through the powerful spoken word that goes forth ahead of us to present itself in due time.

Just a little while longer son, just a little while longer daughter, just a little while longer husband, just a little while longer wife, just a little while longer friend, just a little while longer mother, just a little while longer father, just a little while longer preacher, just a little while longer apostle, just a little while longer.

Pray and seek his face, "And let us not be weary in well doing: for in due season we shall reap, if we faint not. As we have therefore opportunity, let us do good unto all men, especially unto them who are of the household of faith." Galatians 6:9-10 KJV

33 - Scriptures

Motivate:

"Blessed [happy, spiritually prosperous, favored by God] is the man who is steadfast under trial *and* perseveres when tempted; for when he has passed the test *and* been approved, he will receive the [victor's] crown of life which *the Lord* has promised to those who love Him." James 1:12 AMP

Teach:

"See to it that no one takes you captive through philosophy and empty deception [pseudo-intellectual babble], according to the tradition [and musings] of *mere* men, following the elementary principles of this world, rather than following [the truth—the teachings of] Christ." Colossians 2:8 AMP

Win:

"For I the Lord thy God will hold thy right hand, saying unto thee, Fear not; I will help thee." Isaiah 41:13 KJV

Trust:

"Trust in and rely confidently on the Lord with all your heart and do not rely on your own insight or understanding. In all your ways know and acknowledge and recognize Him, And He will make your paths straight and smooth [removing obstacles that block your way]." Proverbs 3:5-6 AMP

Fear-Not:

"But He knows the way that I take [and He pays attention to it]. *When* He has tried me, I will come forth as [refined] gold [pure and luminous]." Job 23:10 AMP

Shift: _____

"No temptation [regardless of its source] has overtaken *or* enticed you that is not common to human experience [nor is any temptation unusual or beyond human resistance]; but God is faithful [to His word—He is compassionate and trustworthy], and He will not let you be tempted beyond your ability [to resist], but along with the temptation He [has in the past and is now and] will [always] provide the way out as well, so that you will be able to endure it [without yielding, and will overcome temptation with joy]." 1 Corinthians 10:13 AMP

Devotional # 34

Nothing is Too Hard for God

"Ah, Sovereign Lord, you have made the heavens and the earth by your great power and outstretched arm. Nothing is too hard for you." Jeremiah 32:17 NIV

34 - Scriptures

Motivate: _____

"But seek ye first the kingdom of God, and his righteousness; and all these things shall be added unto you." Matthew 6:33 KJV

Teach: _____

"The things [the doctrine, the precepts, the admonitions, the sum of my ministry] which you have heard me teach in the presence of many witnesses, entrust [as a treasure] to reliable and faithful men who will also be capable and qualified to teach others." 2 Timothy 2:2 AMP

Win: _____

"Bring all the tithes (the tenth) into the storehouse, so that there may be food in My house, and test Me now in this," says the Lord of hosts, "if I will not open for you the windows of heaven and pour out for you [so great] a blessing until there is no more room to receive it." Malachi 3:10 AMP

Trust: _____

"The Lord is good, A strength and stronghold in the day of trouble; He knows [He recognizes, cares for, and understands fully] those who take refuge and trust in Him." Nahum 1:7 AMP

Fear-Not: _____

"Even though I walk through the [sunless] valley of the shadow of death, I fear no evil, for You are with me; Your rod [to protect] and Your staff [to guide], they comfort and console me." Psalm 23:4 AMP

Shift: _____

"For God hath not given us the spirit of fear; but of power, and of love, and of a sound mind." 2 Timothy 1:7 KJV

Devotional # 35
Don't Feed the Symptom

We all have our ways of behavior, conduct and attitude. But have you noticed that when we come into the presence of others who display ways that may be similar or even more dominant than ours that we tend to make a conscious decision to modify or suppress some of our ways in order to facilitate theirs? We may find ourselves talking differently, moving differently, and even thinking differently in order to make the environment peaceful.

Sometimes we may find that we have to hold our tongue a lot and humble ourselves, just to get by in the moment. But the truth remains that "… on the day of judgment people will have to give an accounting for every careless or useless word they speak. For by your words [reflecting your spiritual condition] you will be justified and acquitted of the guilt of sin; and by your words [rejecting Me] you will be condemned and sentenced." Matthew 12:36-37 AMP

Truly our words are not something that we should handle carelessly. The bible says, "Whoever guards his mouth and tongue Keeps his soul from troubles." Proverbs 21:23 NKJV. But some may think that because we choose to guard our mouth to keep us out of trouble that that in itself is enough. But when we internalize the very unspeakable words and negativity towards others, we end up feeding the symptoms of bitterness, anger, animosity, and/or resentment which ultimately manifests itself outwardly "… along with every kind of malice [all spitefulness, verbal abuse, malevolence]." Ephesians 4:31 AMP

God doesn't want our minds, hearts, spirits, and our souls to linger in this state of unrest. He has called us, chosen us, and he has many promises in store for us. But until we get it together, he waits. He waits for the many who allow their of state of mind toward others to trap them in the prison of their minds. Confined to the symptomatic feelings of a mental state that manifests itself, creating many outward conditions that contradicts the foretold promises of God.

It is important that we always remember that God "...does not delay [as though He were unable to act] and is not slow about His promise, as some count slowness, but is [extraordinarily] patient toward you, not wishing for any to perish but for all to come to repentance." 2 Peter 3:9 AMP

We're the ones that are taking too long to surrender it all to him and to fall in line. The bible encourages us to "...live a life worthy of the calling to which you have been called [that is, to live a life that exhibits godly character, moral courage, personal integrity, and mature behavior—a life that expresses gratitude to God for your salvation], with all humility [forsaking self-righteousness], and gentleness [maintaining self-control], with patience, bearing with one another in [unselfish] love." Ephesians 4:1-2 AMP.

The Lord teaches us how to forgive and let go, how to maintain and reclaim, how to love in-spite of, how to use understanding and wisdom to adapt new ways, and new skills of interacting, processing and producing productive effective solutions. Don't allow the issues of life to fester. Don't feed the symptoms! "Make every effort to keep the oneness of the Spirit in the bond of peace [each individual working together to make the whole successful]." Ephesians 4:3 AMP

35 - Scriptures

Motivate: _____

"A soothing tongue [speaking words that build up and encourage] is a tree of life, but a perversive tongue [speaking words that overwhelm and depress] crushes the spirit." Proverbs 15:4 AMP

Teach: _____

"If anyone thinks himself to be religious [scrupulously observant of the rituals of his faith], and does not control his tongue but deludes his own heart, this person's religion is worthless (futile, barren)." James 1:26 AMP

Win: _____

"If you want to enjoy life and see many happy days, keep your tongue from speaking evil and your lips from telling lies." 1 Peter 3:10 NLT

Trust: _____

"Death and life are in the power of the tongue, And those who love it and indulge it will eat its fruit and bear the consequences of their words." Proverbs 18:21 AMP

Fear-Not: _____

"… whatever goes into the mouth passes into the stomach, and is eliminated? But whatever [word] comes out of the mouth comes from the heart, and this is what defiles and dishonors the man." Matthew 15:17-18 AMP

Shift: _____

"Do not let unwholesome [foul, profane, worthless, vulgar] words ever come out of your mouth, but only such speech as is good for building up others, according to the need and the occasion, so that it will be a blessing to those who hear [you speak]." Ephesians 4:29 AMP

Devotional # 36

Give Up? ... Nah!

Even when you think you are losing faith in the things that matter to you, all you need to do is push through.

Feeling defeated can be easily shaken off if we don't succumb to the symptoms that it lets on. Even in our speaking, if we continuously speak positive words of affirmation, we can intercept our negative thought process, every single time it seems takes flight.

Symptoms are real and our is body trained to physically react to our mind's perspective. The Bible says, "There is surely a future hope for you, and your hope will not be cut off." Proverbs 23:18 NIV

So, keep moving, believing and pursuing. Keep releasing, gaining, and sustaining.

"Let us not become weary in doing good, for at the proper time we will reap a harvest if we do not give up." Galatians 6:9 NIV

36 - Scriptures

Motivate: _____

"But you, take courage! Do not let your hands be weak, for your work shall be rewarded." 2 Chronicles 15:7 ESV

Teach: _____

"I must work the works of him that sent me, while it is day: the night cometh, when no man can work." John 9:4 KJV

Win: _____

"I press on to reach the end of the race and receive the heavenly prize for which God, through Christ Jesus, is calling us." Philippians 3:14 NLT

Trust: _____

"Follow peace with all men, and holiness, without which no man shall see the Lord:" Hebrews 12:14 KJV

Fear-Not: _____

"Do not let your heart be troubled (afraid, cowardly). Believe [confidently] in God and trust in Him, [have faith, hold on to it, rely on it, keep going and] believe also in Me." John 14:1 AMP

Shift: _____

"In My Father's house are many dwelling places. If it were not so, I would have told you, because I am going there to prepare a place for you. And if I go and prepare a place for you, I will come back again and I will take you to Myself, so that where I am you may be also. And [to the place] where I am going, you know the way." John 14:2-4 AMP

Devotional # 37

Forgetting Forgiveness?

"Be kind and compassionate to one another, forgiving each other, just as in Christ God forgave you." Ephesians 4:32 NIV

Sometimes we are extremely hard on ourselves when we think back on the things that we've done, said, or even thought. We begin to behave as if we've forgotten that we've been forgiven. Sadly, there are also times when we behave as if our brothers and sisters have not been forgiven either.

When we recall the things that others have done in the past, we can begin to treat others in a way that we shouldn't (almost as if we are still holding them in bondage for their past sins).

The crazy thing about this mind that God has given us, is that we constantly have the capability to easily remember the good as well as the bad. But we have a responsibility to keep the sins of the past from negatively affecting our future. When we recall bad memories (whether about others or ourselves) we need to ensure that we seek to make them effective toward our current life today as well as our future life tomorrow. A good way to do so is to refer to our past sin as 'the test'. Did we pass or fail it? Was any part of it within our control, which could have possibly yielded a different outcome? Could we have done anything differently? Did we learn anything from it? Have we met or come across anyone in life that our test can be considered a study guide for them? Has our experience grown and matured us? Do we acknowledge the role that factors like emotional, social, economic, spiritual, mental, personal maturity and physical factors have contributed to those tests, along with willingness and desire to act accordingly or do what is necessary?

Once we have acknowledged that it was a test, then we can recall how we overcame it by the Grace of God (whether pass or fail); which turns that test into a testimony. Those testimonies can effectively be used towards our salvation instead of letting the recollection of our sin cause us to sink into a dark place.

Tests where we feel we may have failed or fell short, are things to consider praying about and possibly even seeking proper counsel on. We can ask God to show us, teach us, and guide us so that we can have a testimony, rather than just the pain of the situation that may seem to keep on occurring and we don't know or understand why.

Psalm 25:4-7 NIV says "Show me your ways, Lord, teach me your paths. Guide me in your truth and teach me, for you are God my Savior, and my hope is in you all day long. Remember, Lord, your great mercy and love, for they are from of old. Do not remember the sins of my youth and my rebellious ways; according to your love remember me, for you, Lord, are good."

God has truly been merciful unto salvation. And because of his great love we can continue to hope for a brighter day and a brighter tomorrow. We constantly ask him for forgiveness, and he is faithful to giving us new mercies and a clean slate, day by day. God remembers us; and if we remember him the way that he remembers us, (minute by minute, moment by moment, hour by hour, event by event, issue by issue, blessing by blessing, and day by day), life will be a whole lot different.

Psalm 77:11-14 NIV says, ["I will remember the deeds of the Lord; yes, I will remember your miracles of long ago. I will consider all your works and meditate on all your mighty deeds." Your ways, God, are holy. What god is as great as our God? You are the God who performs miracles; you display your power among the peoples.]

My prayer: Lord help me to not forget your forgiveness but to remember your good deeds, your miracles, all the times that you brought me out. Help me to remember that it is because of your great love for me that I can take a stand on Holy ground with my sins forgiven, and that I can look upon others in the same manner. And in all situations, I can know without a doubt, that you are good, because I am not condemned, for your mercies are new day by day, your mercies are true and faithful, and your mercies endureth forever. Thank you for Salvation.

Amen.

37 - Scriptures

Motivate: _____

"Be kind and helpful to one another, tender-hearted [compassionate, understanding], forgiving one another [readily and freely], just as God in Christ also forgave you." Ephesians 4:32 AMP

Teach: _____

"Then Peter came to Him and asked, "Lord, how many times will my brother sin against me and I forgive him and let it go? Up to seven times?" Jesus answered him, "I say to you, not up to seven times, but seventy times seven." Matthew 18:21-22 AMP

Win: _____

"Whenever you stand praying, if you have anything against anyone, forgive him [drop the issue, let it go], so that your Father who is in heaven will also forgive you your transgressions and wrongdoings [against Him and others]." Mark 11:25 AMP

Trust: _____

"He has not dealt with us according to our sins [as we deserve], Nor rewarded us [with punishment] according to our wickedness." Psalm 103:10-14 AMP

Fear-Not: _____

"For as the heavens are high above the earth, so great is His lovingkindness toward those who fear and worship Him [with awe-filled respect and deepest reverence]." Psalm 103:10-14 AMP

Shift: _____

"As far as the east is from the west, so far has He removed our transgressions from us." Psalm 103:10-14 AMP

Devotional # 38

Sharing Understanding

Understanding is something that is necessary, but not everyone grasps it the same way. In life we will constantly find ourselves in the position where we have to explain things to others. And regardless of the topic, depending on the willingness of each side to 'unfold their words', meaning rephrase, reword, express or put things differently so that it can be understood, it can sometimes bring frustration, anger, and many other ill feelings. A lack of understanding can even harden ones heart to some things because of the inability to grasp a concept thereby hindering their ability to accept.

Psalm 119 ESV talks about how the Lord's Word is a Lamp to our feet. It means that as we go about life, the light of our way is in the effective knowledge and manifestation of his word, that he has given to us in understanding. Verse 130 says "The unfolding of your words gives light; it imparts understanding to the simple."

Patience is one of the fruits of the spirit that is often required depending on the length of the process in the unfolding of our words. Colossians 4:6 ESV says "Let your speech always be gracious, seasoned with salt, so that you may know how you ought to answer each person."

The Lord has led the way by being our prime example so that we can follow his ways effectively. But to do so we have to use his tools as well.

"Hear, O children, the instruction of a father, and pay attention [and be willing to learn] so that you may gain understanding and intelligent discernment. For I give you good doctrine; Do not turn away from my instruction." Proverbs 4:1-2 AMP

"Get wisdom! Get understanding! Do not forget, nor turn away from the words of my mouth. Do not forsake her, and she will preserve you; Love her, and she will keep you. Wisdom is the principal thing; Therefore get wisdom. And in all your getting, get understanding. Exalt her, and she will promote you; She will bring you honor, when you embrace her. She will place on your head an ornament of grace; A crown of glory she will deliver to you." Hear, my son, and receive my sayings, And the years of your life will be many." Proverbs 4:5-10 NKJV

38 - Scriptures

Motivate: _____

"My son, if you will receive my words and treasure my commandments within you, So that your ear is attentive to [skillful and godly] wisdom, And apply your heart to understanding [seeking it conscientiously and striving for it eagerly];" Proverbs 2:1-2 AMP

Teach: _____

"Yes, if you cry out for insight, and lift up your voice for understanding; If you seek skillful and godly wisdom as you would silver and search for her as you would hidden treasures;" Proverbs 2:3-4 AMP

Win: _____

"Then you will understand the [reverent] fear of the Lord [that is, worshiping Him and regarding Him as truly awesome] And discover the knowledge of God." Proverbs 2:5 AMP

Trust: _____

"For the Lord gives [skillful and godly] wisdom; From His mouth come knowledge and understanding." Proverbs 2:6 AMP

Fear-Not: _____

"He stores away sound wisdom for the righteous [those who are in right standing with Him]; He is a shield to those who walk in integrity [those of honorable character and moral courage]," Proverbs 2:7 AMP

Shift: _____

"He guards the paths of justice; And He preserves the way of His saints (believers). Then you will understand righteousness and justice [in every circumstance] And integrity and every good path. For [skillful and godly] wisdom will enter your heart and knowledge will be pleasant to your soul. Discretion will watch over you, Understanding and discernment will guard you," Proverbs 2:8-11 AMP

Devotional # 39

Mature Acceptance

"May the God who gives endurance and encouragement give you the same attitude of mind toward each other that Christ Jesus had, so that with one mind and one voice you may glorify the God and Father of our Lord Jesus Christ. Accept one another, then, just as Christ accepted you, in order to bring praise to God." Romans 15:5-7 NIV

If there is one area that we have all been challenged in, it is acceptance. Whether in school, at work, in sports, social gatherings, among family, friends, and even in church, we all have encountered the issue of acceptance.

Acceptance is something that everyone wants to have to some extent, even if some act as if they don't care about it, or don't need it. Others seemingly demand it by being outgoing, extra, and boisterous. They need to stand out to draw attention, they feed off of being the life of the party, and they look for a response for gratification and wear it proudly on their sleeves.

It really isn't that hard to get swept into our feelings and into the sense of a desire for acceptance. Many don't just post things on social media and don't desire to see who viewed it and how many comments and likes they've received. We crave the acceptance, and we tally it up. We even evaluate which kinds of posts will bring us an even greater following and liking.

If not from people, we desire acceptance from animals, pets, or anything that can bring us that sense of attention. We desire it from our environment, the places we go. We even desire it from the earth, the land and the sea. When we plant a seed, we desire the land to accept it and we wait for a response by seeing the growth. When we go fishing, we desire for the fish to accept our bait and we will sit around for hours just waiting and hoping that they would be fooled and take a bite.

We get such a deeply gratifying feeling from acceptance that we don't always respond with gratitude because it is so built into our nature. We expect acceptance because we know what responses our signals can and should produce, and when it doesn't measure up to that expectation, frustration, animosity, and negativity can arise.

But acceptance is not a just a feeling of harmony where everyone is on the same song-sheet in one accord: Yay or Nay. There is a Melody that goes with Acceptance. When we put on the mind of Christ, we can begin to understand that the Acceptance the Bible talks about is achieved through Spiritual maturity. It is not a feeling but rather an attitude of the Mind of Christ that we are members of one body, and we have need of each other.

The Bible says, in Philippians 2:5-6 KJV, "Let this mind be in you, which was also in Christ Jesus: Who, being in the form of God, thought it not robbery to be equal with God".

When you accept Jesus as your Lord and savior and don't just stop there, but you actually proceed to study his word and show yourself approved to him as one who is available to be used by him; there is a special anointing that is placed on your life that encourages you to continue to try your best and even if you fall short, it causes you to press through and live your life with the guidance of the Lord, laying aside your will for his. This is what it means when you let the mind of the Spirit be in you which is also in Christ Jesus.

Christ has given up his life in place of ours so that our entry into the gates of heaven will be accepted since he lives in us, because he cannot deny himself. And that exchange is also not considered robbery from the equality of who Christ is in the form of God (the Spirit) who is the mind of the Spirit. Rather he has given us a portion of himself (a measure based on our capacity) and anything that carries a portion of something/someone greater is considered a descendant, a successor, a progeny, an offspring. For "in him we live and move and have our being; ... For we are indeed his offspring." (Acts 17:28 ESV). And that lifeblood of the Holy Spirit is the very reason we are considered sons and daughters of the most high.

The Bible tells us in 1 Peter 1:12 that even the angels desire to look into what we have.

How humbling it is to know that while we are desiring acceptance from everything and everyone around us; that **Heaven desires our acceptance**.

As children of God, we are **called TO accept** one another, **NOT to seek acceptance** from each other, but instead seeking acceptance from God. So then, "May the God who gives endurance and encouragement give you the same attitude of mind toward each other that Christ Jesus had, so that with one mind and one voice you may glorify the God and Father of our Lord Jesus Christ. Accept one another, then, just as Christ accepted you, in order to bring praise to God." Romans 15:5-7 NIV

39 - Scriptures

Motivate: _____

"I solemnly charge you in the presence of God and of Christ Jesus, who is to judge the living and the dead, and by His appearing and His kingdom: preach the word [as an official messenger]; be ready when the time is right and even when it is not [keep your sense of urgency, whether the opportunity seems favorable or unfavorable, whether convenient or inconvenient, whether welcome or unwelcome]; correct [those who err in doctrine or behavior], warn [those who sin], exhort and encourage [those who are growing toward spiritual maturity], with inexhaustible patience and [faithful] teaching." 2 Timothy 4:1-2 AMP

Teach: _____

"Study and do your best to present yourself to God approved, a workman [tested by trial] who has no reason to be ashamed, accurately handling and skillfully teaching the word of truth. "2 Timothy 2:15 AMP

Win: _____

"Tax collectors and other notorious sinners often came to listen to Jesus teach. This made the Pharisees and teachers of religious law complain that he was associating with such sinful people—even eating with them! So Jesus told them this story: "If a man has a hundred sheep and one of them gets lost, what will he do? Won't he leave the ninety-nine others in the wilderness and go to search for the one that is lost until he finds it?" Luke 15:1-4 NLT

Trust: _____

"And when he has found it, he will joyfully carry it home on his shoulders. When he arrives, he will call together his friends and neighbors, saying, 'Rejoice with me because I have found my lost sheep.' In the same way, there is more joy in heaven over one lost sinner who repents and returns to God than over ninety-nine others who are righteous and haven't strayed away!" Luke 15:5-7 NLT

Fear-Not: _____

"Therefore I tell you, do not be anxious about your life, what you will eat or what you will drink, nor about your body, what you will put on. Is not life more than food, and the body more than clothing?" Matthew 6:25-32 ESV

Shift: _____

"May the God of hope fill you with all joy and peace as you trust in him, so that you may overflow with hope by the power of the Holy Spirit. I myself am convinced, my brothers and sisters, that you yourselves are full of goodness, filled with knowledge and competent to instruct one another." Romans 15:13-14 NIV

Devotional # 40

The Early Bird Catches the Worm

There is something that goes on early in the morning. A period of condensation when water vapor changes to a liquid form. It saturates the surface of the earth and causes the worms to come up to the surface and the Early Bird Catches the Worm.

Zechariah 8:12 KJV says, "For the seed shall be prosperous; the vine shall give her fruit, and the ground shall give her increase, and the heavens shall give their dew; and I will cause the remnant of this people to possess all these things."

How amazing it is for the Lord to declare these things over our lives here on earth and even greater for the heavens to give us their dew. What purity, what a refresh, what mercy he has laid upon us. It is new every morning. Every morning the ground is saturated with his dew. And the early bird gets to reap of that abundant blessing.

Saturate us Lord. Speak Lord, Speak to us. The Remnant is ready to receive.

Rise up in the saturation of the holy spirit and bask in the renewing power of his marvelous glory. He has so many things to say to you.

40 - Scriptures

Motivate: _____

"And it shall come to pass in the last days, saith God, I will pour out of my Spirit upon all flesh: and your sons and your daughters shall prophesy, and your young men shall see visions, and your old men shall dream dreams:" Acts 2:17 KJV

Teach: _____

"But you will receive power and ability when the Holy Spirit comes upon you; and you will be My witnesses [to tell people about Me] both in Jerusalem and in all Judea, and Samaria, and even to the ends of the earth." Acts 1:8 AMP

Win: _____

"If you will turn and pay attention to my rebuke, Behold, I [Wisdom] will pour out my spirit on you; I will make my words known to you." Proverbs 1:23 AMP

Trust: _____

"But the [Holy] Spirit explicitly and unmistakably declares that in later times some will turn away from the faith, paying attention instead to deceitful and seductive spirits and doctrines of demons, [misled] by the hypocrisy of liars whose consciences are seared as with a branding iron [leaving them incapable of ethical functioning], who forbid marriage and advocate abstaining from [certain kinds of] foods which God has created to be gratefully shared by those who believe and have [a clear] knowledge of the truth. For everything God has created is good, and nothing is to be rejected if it is received with gratitude; for it is sanctified [set apart, dedicated to God] by means of the word of God and prayer." 1 Timothy 4:1-5 AMP

Fear-Not: _____

"Children, it is the last hour [the end of this age]; and just as you heard that the antichrist is coming [the one who will oppose Christ and attempt to replace Him], even now many antichrists (false teachers) have appeared, which confirms our belief that it is the last hour." 1 John 2:18 AMP

Shift: _____

"For there the seed will produce peace and prosperity; the vine will yield its fruit, and the ground will produce its increase, and the heavens will give their dew. And I will cause the remnant of this people to inherit and possess all these things." Zechariah 8:12 AMP

Devotional # 41

Speak Up, Not Down

"Let no corrupting talk come out of your mouths, but only such as is good for building up, as fits the occasion, that it may give grace to those who hear." Ephesians 4:29 ESV

Speaking down is easy, thoughtless and even feeds that side of us that believes that our freedom to speak comes without limits. That rebellious nature, that instinctively speaks first and processes later. But Speaking Up is a responsibility and usually is spoken from a responsible person.

Speaking Up is building, uplifting, edifying, teaching, educating, boosting, and elevating each other to a higher state of Character. Not only does the bible tell us to speak what is good for building up, but it also says to speak "as fits the occasion".

There are many ways we can Speak Up to others, but it doesn't mean that it always or even immediately helps them. Sometimes we can Speak Up to others and it doesn't even interest them or is in any way immediately useful to them in their current lifestyle or mindset. 1 Corinthians 10:23 AMP says, "All things are lawful [that is, morally legitimate, permissible], but not all things are beneficial or advantageous. All things are lawful, but not all things are constructive [to character] and edifying [to spiritual life]."

When the scripture says, "All things are lawful", this does not take into account things that are not lawful because we, as people, are held accountable and are expected to operate according to the law, what is generally accepted as right, and what is proper according to our places of residence (whether Christians or not). So, the scripture is merely explaining that while we operate in that truth of lawfulness (because we are within what is right/good), we also need to acknowledge that not all those things are beneficial for us nor builds us up as an individual. So if we are in tune with the environment, culture, community, mindset, emotional, social, statistical, economical, spiritual and many different areas that affect each of us differently, then we are able to interpret our words to what best fits the opportunity or the moment, so that our words can be an asset to the hearer and they can prosper from it.

Therefore, Speaking Up is a two-edged sword. We can build others because we're being built. We can educate others because we're being educated. We can uplift others because we've been uplifted. But for it to be a help and be beneficial to others, we must do so as it fits the occasion. And that's how it gives grace to those who hear it; because we are speaking not just from experience, education, and insight, but we are also speaking with understanding, wisdom, and consideration (careful thought, examination or study of how to apply).

41 - Scriptures

Motivate: _____

"Therefore encourage one another and build one another up, just as you are doing." 1 Thessalonians 5:11 ESV

Teach: _____

"And if you do not carry your own cross and follow me, you cannot be my disciple." Luke 14:27 NLT

Win: _____

"For which of you, desiring to build a tower, does not first sit down and count the cost, whether he has enough to complete it??" Luke 14:28 ESV

Trust: _____

"For we are both God's workers. And you are God's field. You are God's building. Because of God's grace to me, I have laid the foundation like an expert builder. Now others are building on it." 1 Corinthians 3:9-10 NLT

Fear-Not: _____

"But whoever is building on this foundation must be very careful. For no one can lay any foundation other than the one we already have—Jesus Christ." 1 Corinthians 3:10-11 NLT

Shift: _____

"Anyone who builds on that foundation may use a variety of materials—gold, silver, jewels, wood, hay, or straw. But on the judgment day, fire will reveal what kind of work each builder has done. The fire will show if a person's work has any value. If the work survives, that builder will receive a reward. But if the work is burned up, the builder will suffer great loss. The builder will be saved, but like someone barely escaping through a wall of flames." 1 Corinthians 3:9-15 NLT

Devotional # 42

Edification Speaks

Have you ever been in a place of worship/church and notice some members or church goers or even leaders seem so high minded that they can't even connect with worship, praise, prayer, or the word? It can be even the most touching of moments where it is obvious that the fire of the Holy Spirit just moved through the place, but such individuals just choose to either oversee and observe proudly in approval and sanction of what is going on or would be the first to boldly disapprove, oppose or reject in an open and scornful manner; not considering that their approach can be considered disrespectful and impolite. In some cases, their actions can even deter others from not wanting to fellowship in such place(s), and even discourage and put a blockage or change in other hearts towards their personal view of the church as a whole.

Wow. It is truly amazing the effect that just one can have on a multitude. Many can attest to seeing this behavior in many churches across the world. Depending on the position, title or status of such impactful and influential persons, the effects can be devastating in such that it can affect the growth and stability of the church in multiple areas and functions. It truly is an elephant in the room that can make God's people appear blind and bound, because it reduces the impact of the authentic and unhindered manifestation of the blessings of the Holy Spirit.

We cannot lose focus on the purpose of the Church and the Grace that has brought us into our New Testament and new dispensation (appointment, inheritance, governing and covering authority). Edification is vital to the healthy blood pressure of the church, ensuring that the precious blood of Jesus that is pumped by the heartbeat of the Holy Spirit is effective to ALL members. Not just to thrive and survive but to overcome and prosper in the plans that God has for each of us to the building up of the church as one body.

If we give each other the benefit of the doubt, we will see that many of those same individuals have underlying good intentions for the church and the Lord's people. An even closer look can further reveal a series of personal sacrifices made for the acquisition, establishment and building of many places of worship all throughout the earth, as well as sacrifices of family, time, resources and labor.

But regardless if how good or great our intentions and sacrifices are, we must be mindful that our approach, words and actions can easily become misconstrued and misinterpreted to mean something that we didn't intend and thereby can appear to render our current and past contributions as ineffective, causing our works to be cast aside, and disregarded because it is unrecognizable (to those who hear it) as something of edification that gives Grace. The bible says "... Behold, to obey is better than sacrifice, And to heed [is better] than the fat of rams." 1 Samuel 15:22 AMP. "Let no corrupting talk come out of your mouths, but only such as is good for building up, as fits the occasion, that it may give grace to those who hear." Ephesians 4:29 ESV.

The interpretation of those that hear what we say and do is of great importance to God, despite our intentions. "But speaking the truth in love [in all things—both our speech and our lives expressing His truth], let us grow up in all things into Him [following His example] who is the Head—Christ. From Him the whole body [the church, in all its various parts], joined and knitted firmly together by what every joint supplies, when each part is working properly, causes the body to grow and mature, building itself up in [unselfish] love." Ephesians 4:15-16 AMP

Edification Speaks loudly and interprets the move of the Holy Spirit, revealing God's love and Grace that nurtures, sustains, and builds, keeping us humble, receptive and partakers of the fruits of the spirit.

"Remind the people of these facts, and solemnly charge them in the presence of God to avoid petty controversy over words, which does no good, and [upsets and undermines and] ruins [the faith of] those who listen. Study and do your best to present yourself to God approved, a workman [tested by trial] who has no reason to be ashamed, accurately handling and **skillfully** teaching the word of truth." 2 Timothy 2:14-15 AMP

42 - Scriptures

Motivate: _____

"Let no corrupting talk come out of your mouths, but only such as is good for building up, as fits the occasion, that it may give grace to those who hear." Ephesians 4:29 ESV

Teach: _____

"So then, let us pursue [with enthusiasm] the things which make for peace and the building up of one another [things which lead to spiritual growth]." Romans 14:19 AMP

Win: _____

"When you meet together, each one has a psalm, a teaching, a revelation (disclosure of special knowledge), a tongue, or an interpretation. Let everything be constructive and edifying and done for the good of all the church." 1 Corinthians 14:26 AMP

Trust: _____

"He who descended is the very same as He who also has ascended high above all the heavens, that He [His presence] might fill all things [that is, the whole universe])." Ephesians 4:10 AMP

Fear-Not: _____

"And [His gifts to the church were varied and] He Himself appointed some as apostles [special messengers, representatives], some as prophets [who speak a new message from God to the people], some as evangelists [who spread the good news of salvation], and some as pastors and teachers [to shepherd and guide and instruct]," Ephesians 4:11 AMP

Shift: _____

"[and He did this] to fully equip and perfect the saints (God's people) for works of service, to build up the body of Christ [the church]; until we all reach oneness in the faith and in the knowledge of the Son of God, [growing spiritually] to become a mature believer, reaching to the measure of the fullness of Christ [manifesting His spiritual completeness and exercising our spiritual gifts in unity]. So that we are no longer children [spiritually immature], tossed back and forth [like ships on a stormy sea] and carried about by every wind of [shifting] doctrine, by the cunning and trickery of [unscrupulous] men, by the deceitful scheming of people ready to do anything [for personal profit]. But speaking the truth in love [in all things—both our speech and our lives expressing His truth], let us grow up in all things into Him [following His example] who is the Head—Christ." Ephesians 4:12-15 AMP

Devotional # 43

My Idiosyncrasy!

An idiosyncrasy is a unique and distinctive behavior that is generally exclusive or identifiable to you and is mostly recognized and made fond of by those in your circle(s). You may have a snort when you laugh, or you may always sneeze as soon as you begin to eat; or you may have a special thing that you do when you're in your thinking mode, or that particular way you act when you are extremely tired. You may even have a quirky thing that you do when you're excited. You may pass-gas or hick-up when you're nervous, or burp when your back is rubbed, or wrestle with your feet or hands under the table when you don't know what to say or do next. Some idiosyncrasies can be so bizarre that it can truly create the most authentic of relationships and some can be so off-the-wall that it can constantly put those around you to the test.

An idiosyncrasy that is identifiable to you, doesn't mean that you are the only one in the world that has that specific behavior to that precise thing. There are communities and groups for almost everything these days for people who share "weird", normal or just similar things in common.

Are you aware of your own idiosyncrasies or the ones others have made you aware of? Do you acknowledge that you do them or are you in denial? Are you proud of them or sometimes embarrassed by them? Have you ever thought about whether or not your idiosyncrasies hurt you or helps you? Have you considered whether or not your idiosyncrasies draw others to you or sends people in the opposite direction?

Life can be very push and pull, give and take, stretched and loosed, bound and free. And that can leave us in a place where we don't know whether those peculiarities enable our freedom or subjects us to bondage.

Some idiosyncrasies that one may think defines us can be voluntary or involuntary. But regardless of how it comes about, it can be very disadvantageous to only validate ourselves by those behaviors. Our distinctive mannerisms can derive from learned or created habits and even reactions and exposure to our environments, experiences or people who have contributed or played a major role in shaping who we are. It is especially notable by our words that either validate or condemn those behaviors.

But at some point, we have to draw a line between who we are as a whole and the idiosyncrasies that seemingly classify, group or define portions of who we are. We have to divide what actually benefits us from what holds us back.

Who we are is much greater than the self we currently know and much deeper than the things that others or even we ourselves can't seem to get past, at times. Applying wisdom, shows us a glimpse of the bigger picture.

Our idiosyncrasies should not define who we are, but should rather, overtime, create historical moments over the course of our lives that can be talked about in reverence, connecting and bridging gaps of uncommonness with noteworthy, peculiar people (like yourself) for generations to come. Our idiosyncrasies are not the essence, core, lifeblood, spirit, soul or substance of our workmanship (all that went into our creation to accomplish our reason for existence); For we are a master work of art, spiritually transformed and renewed and well equipped to walk into the path of life that God has already prepared and made ready for us to walk into. But, our idiosyncrasies, are rather impressions that are carved into our craftmanship that shows up on the design feature of our artistry, expressive and identifiable, setting us apart and therefore demonstrating the peculiarity, uniqueness and individuality of our skillful workmanship.

"But ye are a chosen generation, a royal priesthood, an holy nation, **a peculiar people**; that ye should shew forth the praises of him who hath called you out of darkness into his marvellous light;" 1 Peter 2:9 KJV.

43 - Scriptures

Motivate: _____

"He who overcomes [the world by adhering faithfully to Christ Jesus as Lord and Savior] will inherit these things, and I will be his God and he will be My son." Revelation 21:7 AMP

Teach: _____

"For we are His workmanship [His own master work, a work of art], created in Christ Jesus [reborn from above—spiritually transformed, renewed, ready to be used] for good works, which God prepared [for us] beforehand [taking paths which He set], so that we would walk in them [living the good life which He prearranged and made ready for us]." Ephesians 2:10 AMP

Win: _____

"But to as many as did receive and welcome Him, He gave the right [the authority, the privilege] to become children of God, that is, to those who believe in (adhere to, trust in, and rely on) His name—" John 1:12 AMP

Trust: _____

"And I will be a Father to you, and you will be My sons and daughters," Says the Lord Almighty." 2 Corinthians 6:18 AMP

Fear-Not: _____

"See how very much our Father loves us, for he calls us his children, and that is what we are! But the people who belong to this world don't recognize that we are God's children because they don't know him." 1 John 3:1 NLT

Shift: _____

"Because you are precious in My sight, You are honored and I love you" Isaiah 43:4 AMP

CONTROL & AFFECT

PART III

Devotional #'s 44-52

"Out of the same mouth come both blessing and cursing. These things, my brothers, should not be this way [for we have a moral obligation to speak in a manner that reflects our fear of God and profound respect for His precepts]."

James 3:10 AMP

Devotional # 44
Concepts to Basis

"But as for you, continue in what you have learned and have become convinced of, because you know those from whom you learned it, and how from infancy you have known the Holy Scriptures, which are able to make you wise for salvation through faith in Christ Jesus."
2 Timothy 3:14-15 NIV

Learning is a part of life that is involuntary. It is the receipt of information by using our senses of seeing, hearing, touching, smelling, and tasting. For some who lack any of these, the remaining senses tend to heighten its ability in order to compensate for the imbalance. Through our senses we develop concepts which need a basis that has been tested and proven through experience. This can be backed by testimony and wise counsel, which helps us to understand and accept what we consider as real beliefs in our lives.

To remain in the initial stages of our learning (which is the point our senses receive the information) means that we go through life basing our thoughts and actions, only on received feelings that stimulates our initial thoughts. And that is a dangerous place to be in, because it forces us to believe something that we've immediately formed an idea on and causes us to act on it as we see fit, with no advice from anyone else who can validate the information we've learned/received from our senses.

Remaining in this place is what the Bible describes as a fool.

The Bible is very straight forward, precise and spares no firmness of tone to get its message across directly when it comes to counsel, wisdom, and instruction. These are just a few scriptures for reference:

"Listen to advice and accept discipline, and at the end you will be counted among the wise."
Proverbs 19:20 NIV

"Whoever trusts in his own mind is a fool, but he who walks in wisdom will be delivered."
Proverbs 28:26 ESV

"Through pride and presumption come nothing but strife, but [skillful and godly] wisdom is with those who welcome [well-advised] counsel."
Proverbs 13:10 AMP

"The way of fools seems right to them, but the wise listen to advice. Fools show their annoyance at once, but the prudent overlook an insult."
Proverbs 12:15-16 NIV

We all have experienced moments where we've acted impulsively unwise. That doesn't make us fools, just foolish.

Because of the Holy Spirit that resides in us we do not remain in that place. "No one who is born of God will continue to sin, because God's seed remains in them; they cannot go on sinning, because they have been born of God. This is how we know who the children of God are..."
1 John 3:9-10 NIV

We cannot control what we learn because the information we will receive throughout life is vast and unending. Neither can we control our concept in which we try to understand what we observe or experience. What we do have control over is the formation of our basis that lays the foundation of Truth through the resources and tools that God has given us to edify our life **and** the body of Christ. As you do so, "see to it that no one takes you captive through hollow and deceptive philosophy, which depends on human tradition and the elemental spiritual forces of this world rather than on Christ."

Colossians 2:8 NIV "Let perseverance finish its work so that you may be mature and complete, not lacking anything. If any of you lacks wisdom, you should ask God, who gives generously to all without finding fault, and it will be given to you."
James 1:4-5 NIV

Therefore, allow your concepts to be shaped and matured through your basis in Christ.

44 - Scriptures

Motivate: _____

"And blessed [joyful, favored by God] is he who does not take offense at Me [accepting Me as the Messiah and trusting confidently in My message of salvation]." Matthew 11:6 AMP

Teach: _____

"From the days of John the Baptist until now the kingdom of heaven suffers violent assault, and violent men seize it by force [as a precious prize]." Matthew 11:12 AMP

Win: _____

"But be doers of the word, and not hearers only, deceiving yourselves." James 1:22 ESV

Trust: _____

"For the LORD knows *and* fully approves the way of the righteous, But the way of the wicked shall perish." Psalm 1:6 AMP

Fear-Not: _____

[For you did not receive the spirit of slavery to fall back into fear, but you have received the Spirit of adoption as sons, by whom we cry, "Abba! Father!"] Romans 8:15 ESV

Shift: _____

"Blessed [fortunate, prosperous, and favored by God] is the man who does not walk in the counsel of the wicked [following their advice and example], Nor stand in the path of sinners, Nor sit [down to rest] in the seat of scoffers (ridiculers). Psalm 1:1 AMP

Devotional # 45

The Shift is Restricted by the Entanglement

I was looking at a reality show about tow trucks making major tractor trailer rescues on the highways. There was an accident that caused a huge tractor trailer to overturn with some heavy steel coil rolls strapped to its extended flat bed. Usually, it is beneficial to remove additional weight off overturned vehicles for reasons such as lessening the load and reducing the strain on the ropes, straps, or chains as the vehicle is being pulled to its feet. However, in this particular case, there were a number of factors that made removing the tightly strapped coils, more of a hazard than a benefit.

Due to the weight of not only the tractor, but also the weight of the coils, about 3 tow trucks worked together to share the burden so that they can pull the overturned truck back onto its wheels with its load still strapped to it. But something happened during the pull to safety; the weight of the heavy load shifted. The steel coils slid to the edge of the tractor's flatbed putting so much weight on its side, that if the tow trucks released their connections (despite the tractor now being on its own wheels), the tractor would fall right back over again because of the shifted weight pulling it back down.

So, the tow trucks had to stay connected to the tractor trailer and turn their attention towards shifting the coils back to the center of the flat bed so that the weight would become evenly distributed, and the tractor could stand on its own, unsupported.

But that posed another problem.

During the shift of the coils, some of the chains of the tow trucks that were connected to the tractor trailer, got entangled in the chains that were holding the steel coil rolls to the overturned trailer. At this point, it became evident that one of the tow trucks chains needed to be cut in order to release the entanglement.

But with the cut, posed a dangerous issue. There was so much tension on the entangled chains, that if the chain was cut in the wrong place, it would cause it to snap with such great force that it could fatally injure anyone around. So, the chain had to be evaluated and cut at the spot with the least amount of tension, allowing one of the tow trucks chains to be safely released, so that the other chains would become untangled and again strengthened to continue their work.

Because the restriction made by the entanglement was gone, the load was shifted and recentered so that the weight of the coils was again evenly distributed on the back of the tractor trailer, and then the trailer was pulled to its feet.

The tow trucks were finally able to release their chains and the tractor trailer remained on its own wheels with its steel coils still attached.

What a task...

We all carry heavy loads and burdens and sometimes it takes several people praying and/or supporting us in different ways to put us back on our feet when we fall over. Sometimes you may notice that one may have to let go and free themselves from being entangled in our situation, just so that they don't become a restriction to the shift that needs to take place in our lives to put us back on course again.

Whenever someone has released themselves from our situation, if the release is not cut off properly, at the place of least resistance, you may find that there may be a whiplash of tension, anger, resentment, and many other feelings and emotions that affect many involved. And this can drag on and on for days, weeks, months, and even years, depending on each one's level of spiritual maturity. When this happens, the ability for us to see the value in the release, can be obstructed by the present pain and hurt caused by the cut that has left us deeply wounded and the relationship fatally injured (and that's in addition to the current load that we're carrying).

There are times when, intercessors, prayer warriors, ministers, evangelists, apostles, pastors and many others, are tasked with coming in like a tow truck to pull us up with prayer. However, make no mistake, as they attempt to carry another's burdens, lend support, and help however they can, they still have a responsibility to bear their own burdens and personal situations. This can hinder their prayers, support and help to us, especially when our load shifts to the edge and puts too much weight on them, and that's where the real task comes in.

Sometimes freeing themselves is the best thing they can do for us and themselves so that both sides can be free of entanglements.

Other reasons why one may have to release themselves from our situation, can range anywhere from them allowing their personal views, feelings, perception, interpretation, judgement or opinions about our situation, to obstruct the way they help, how they help, how much they help, or if they even choose to help at all. They may also feel like their advice or suggestions aren't being taken seriously, or even being considered as an option by the ones they are trying to help. Other times, one may feel that the situation, tests and/or temps them to potentially fall in the same manner (because of the lack of strength and self-control required to watch themselves), as they attempt to restore us. The Bible says in Galatians 6:1 AMP, "Brothers, if anyone is caught in any sin, you who are spiritual [that is, you who are responsive to the guidance of the Spirit] are to restore such a person in a spirit of gentleness [not with a sense of superiority or self-righteousness], keeping a watchful eye on yourself, so that you are not tempted as well."

As we consider these things, Jesus is our prime example, showing us how we can be released from the restriction of entanglement and therefore free to make the shift to salvation. "Therefore, since we are surrounded by so great a cloud of witnesses [who by faith have testified to the truth of God's absolute faithfulness], stripping off every unnecessary weight and the sin which so easily and cleverly entangles us, let us run with endurance and active persistence the race that is set before us, [looking away from all that will distract us and] focusing our eyes on Jesus, who is the Author and Perfecter of faith [the first incentive for our belief and the One who brings our faith to maturity]…" Hebrews 12:1-2 AMP

45 - Scriptures

Motivate: _____

"Blessed be the Lord, who daily bears us up; God is our salvation. Selah" Psalm 68:19 ESV

Teach: _____

"Carry one another's burdens and in this way, you will fulfill the requirements of the law of Christ [that is, the law of Christian love]." Galatians 6:2 AMP.

Win: _____

"Therefore, since we are surrounded by so great a cloud of witnesses [who by faith have testified to the truth of God's absolute faithfulness], stripping off every unnecessary weight and the sin which so easily and cleverly entangles us, let us run with endurance and active persistence the race that is set before us," Hebrews 12:1 AMP

Trust: _____

"[looking away from all that will distract us and] focusing our eyes on Jesus, who is the Author and Perfecter of faith [the first incentive for our belief and the One who brings our faith to maturity], who for the joy [of accomplishing the goal] set before Him endured the cross, disregarding the shame, and sat down..." Hebrews 12:2 AMP

Fear-Not: _____

"For you did not receive the spirit of slavery to fall back into fear, but you have received the Spirit of adoption as sons, by whom we cry, "Abba! Father!" Romans 8:15 ESV

Shift: _____

"Likewise the Spirit helps us in our weakness. For we do not know what we pray for as we ought, but the Spirit himself intercedes for us with groanings too deep for words. And he who Searches hearts knows what is the mind of the Spirit, because the Spirit intercedes for the saints according to the will of God. And we know that for those who love God all things work together for good, for those who are called according to his purpose." Romans 8:26-28 ESV

Devotional # 46

Peace in the Replacement

In almost every area of life, we notice that there is always someone to take the place of another, always someone to fill in the gap, and always someone waiting in line. When we think that we've come to the end of one chapter or that we're at the place of moving on to another, it is always a good thing to feel a sense of freedom that brings us peace that the work we are leaving behind will be carried on and advanced by someone else.

Sometimes we may find that the people that come after us are more zealous, strong willed and may show signs of accomplishing much more than we did, and there are feelings that can rise up within us causing us to feel many different waves of emotions; especially when they are accepted into the flow of things much quicker and easier than we were, when we started on that path.

Thinking back to when we began our journey, we can recall encounters where we may have struggled to fit in initially, or when we worked together with others that tried to put us through tests to see if we were strong enough to stay the course. And even those times when we messed up and made mistakes and had to build back their trust again. These are all moments that can raise up within us building blocks of resentment, grudges, bitterness, annoyance, and many other irritations towards our replacement. And when we let these feelings fester and it get too far, we can turn a heart of stone towards those who we were once dedicated to, encouraged by, and zealous for, in times past, while unintentionally neglecting to accept the freedom of peace within our hearts that comes with the move, the shift, or the new direction that God is taking us in.

We can become bound by monstrous emotions that threaten to discredit our work, our name, and the memories that we leave behind as we gear up to make our transition. Remember King Saul and David? Saul didn't start out the way we remembered him. What about Moses? Can you imagine if Moses was threatened by his replacement, Joshua? or if Elijah was threatened by his replacement, Elisha? What about John who baptized, he was sent to prepare the way for the Lord Jesus himself. Each one who was appointed to take their place went on to do marvelous things, allowing purpose to bring them into promise, receiving a double portion, connecting the end of physical existence with the beginning of eternal life through the grace of salvation.

The reality is that things won't always go as smoothly as we desire it to go during the transition. There can be a host of frustrations, a rush to get things in place, pressure to teach others all they need to know in a short period of time, and even nervousness as we strive to learn and connect with where we're going.

But the peace that can rest in our hearts, can bring about an attitude that can be valued both to those whom you are leaving behind and to those who are ahead of you.

Only let us stay true to what we have already attained."
Philippians 3:16 AMP.

46 - Scriptures

Motivate: _____

"Not that I have already obtained it [this goal of being Christlike] or have already been made perfect, but I actively press on so that I may take hold of that [perfection] for which Christ Jesus took hold of me and made me His own." Philippians 3:12 AMP

Teach: _____

"Brothers and sisters, I do not consider that I have made it my own yet; but one thing I do: forgetting what lies behind and reaching forward to what lies ahead," Philippians 3:13 AMP

Win: _____

"I press on toward the goal to win the [heavenly] prize of the upward call of God in Christ Jesus." Philippians 3:14 AMP

Trust: _____

"All of us who are mature [pursuing spiritual perfection] should have this attitude. And if in any respect you have a different attitude, that too God will make clear to you." Philippians 3:15 AMP

Fear-Not: _____

"Only let us stay true to what we have already attained." Philippians 3:16 AMP.

Shift: _____

"Brothers and sisters, together follow my example and observe those who live by the pattern we gave you." Philippians 3:17 AMP

Devotional # 47

Life Lesson Moments

"But a certain Samaritan, as he journeyed, came where he was. And when he saw him, he had compassion. So he went to him and bandaged his wounds, pouring on oil and wine; and he set him on his own animal, brought him to an inn, and took care of him. On the next day, when he departed, he took out two denarii, gave them to the innkeeper, and said to him, 'Take care of him; and whatever more you spend, when I come again, I will repay you.'" Luke 10:33-35 NKJV

One thing that we all have in common is that we all have a journey. We all go from one place to the next, physically, mentally, and emotionally. And during our journey's we come across people who appear to be in need. Let's be realistic; sure, there are times in our lives when we've turned a blind eye or ear and just minded our own business, and there are also times that we've looked upon others with compassion but we weren't equipped to help in any way, and it probably made us feel awful. There are also times when we've looked upon others making judgement calls about their situation that God must be repaying them for some wrongdoing in their life.

This Samaritan man came across this man in need; his heart was not only moved by his circumstances, but he was also prepared to help. Not just partially, but completely. First, he bandaged his wounds pouring on oil and wine. Oil has been known to speed up the healing process when applied to wounds. It can also lessen pain, slow down bleeding, reduce inflammation and has many other qualities including the prevention of scar tissue formation allowing the skin cells and tissue to grow. And while oil can heal, wine can be used to clean wounds due to its prominent antioxidant and antiseptic properties. Together oil and wine are a powerful tag team to anyone in need of such aid.

Not only was this Samaritan traveling on his journey with tools for cleansing and healing, but he also was prepared to carry the weight of someone else's load.

How often have we attempted to lend a hand and provide care and upliftment to someone in need, but had no intention of carrying their load? Galatians 6:2 NKJV says "Bear one another's burdens, and so fulfill the law of Christ." Can you imagine if God only treated our wounds and never carried us in times when we couldn't pick ourselves up? Christ didn't only come to show us compassion by cleaning us up, but he came to bear our burdens. Psalm 55:22 NKJV says "Cast your burden on the Lord, And He shall sustain you; ..."

The scripture says that the Samaritan didn't stop at carrying the load of the man, but that he brought the man to an inn and took care of him. Whatever journey this Samaritan was on, he made a decision that this man was important enough to stop what he was doing and where he was going, to give this man his attention. The scripture goes on to tell us that the next day the Samaritan had to leave, but that he left the equivalent of 2 days wages with the innkeeper to take care of the man. The innkeeper was kind enough to further agree to give the Samaritan a line of credit to be repaid upon his return, so that the innkeeper would continue to take care of the man until he was well.

That innkeeper sounds a lot like the Holy Spirit. Christ paid the price to save us and when he had to leave, he sent us the Holy Spirit (an extension of himself), to take care of us and continue the healing and renewal process for as long as it took; day after day, guiding and keeping us. Christ has committed to ensuring our wellbeing by showing love and not leaving us out there to our own fate. He took up our burden and brought us to the inn (the Kingdom, the body of Christ), where we would be taken care of until he returns.

Imagine the difference we can make in others' lives if we are willing to do the same. If we don't just offer to others a temporary fix, but fully attend to the needs of the members of the body of Christ as Christ did for us. I say members because it takes complete trust for a man to go with a stranger to be taken care of, leaving behind fear, anxiety, pride, and disbelief. This man believed in the Samaritan and allowed himself to be moved. What a faith filled moment when we acknowledged that the Lord was passing by, and that he stopped right where we were to help us, and we made the decision to trust and believe. Offering nothing but our lives, we trusted God for healing and renewal.

There is truly a lesson about a life in Christ, granted by the moments we encounter along our journey.

Be prepared.

47 - Scriptures

Motivate: _____

[Jesus came up and said to them, "All authority (all power of absolute rule) in heaven and on earth has been given to Me.] Matthew 28:18 AMP

Teach: _____

"Go therefore and make disciples of all the nations [help the people to learn of Me, believe in Me, and obey My words], baptizing them in the name of the Father and of the Son and of the Holy Spirit, teaching them to observe everything that I have commanded you; …" Matthew 28:19-20 AMP

Win: _____

"… and lo, I am with you always [remaining with you perpetually—regardless of circumstance, and on every occasion], even to the end of the age." Matthew 28:20 AMP

Trust: _____

"For there are many, of whom I have often told you, and now tell you even with tears, who live as enemies of the cross of Christ [rejecting and opposing His way of salvation], whose fate is destruction, whose god is *their* belly [their worldly appetite, their sensuality, their vanity], and *whose* glory is in their shame—who focus their mind on earthly *and* temporal things." Philippians 3:18-19 AMP

Fear-Not: _____

"But [we are different, because] our citizenship is in heaven. And from there we eagerly await [the coming of] the Savior, the Lord Jesus Christ;" Philippians 3:20 AMP

Shift: _____

"Brothers, if anyone is caught in any sin, you who are spiritual [that is, you who are responsive to the guidance of the Spirit] are to restore such a person in a spirit of gentleness [not with a sense of superiority or self-righteousness], keeping a watchful eye on yourself, so that you are not tempted as well. Carry one another's burdens and in this way you will fulfill the requirements of the law of Christ [that is, the law of Christian love]. For if anyone thinks he is something [special] when [in fact] he is nothing [special except in his own eyes], he deceives himself." Galatians 6:1-3 AMP

Devotional # 48

The Great Multitude

To say that 'one doesn't see color' is to say that one is color blind. But the two just don't go together, because even if one only sees black and white, those are still two colors. Recognizing our differences and learning about each other's cultures, replaces fear with respect and builds an awareness toward each other as individuals. But going a step further (out of our comfort zone) embracing new relationships, trying new foods, experiencing different social gatherings, weddings, funerals, and even places of worship, all without the hinderance of scornfulness, pridefulness, arrogance, distaste, disinterest, indifference, disaffection and separation; or setting ourselves apart mentally and/or physically from the idea of welcoming each other (not just as individuals but as a people and a community), is where the real difference comes in.

Appreciation of each other is not just merely tolerating that we share the same space and can relate on general factors of commonness or normalness. Appreciation is deeper than surface acknowledgement. Making a genuine effort to get to know someone, spending time in their presence, and actually finding enjoyment in them (with a recognized gratefulness of the community that has developed and shaped their life), is at the core of appreciation. To appreciate is an understanding that we each have equal worth and value to God, and because of that, we are favored with the privilege of sharing this world together.

Our nativity to different parts of this earth does not negate the reality that we are all a people created from one God who is neither of one race or color or language, but of Spirit. "After this I looked, and there before me was a **Great Multitude** that no one could count, from every nation, tribe, people and language, standing before the throne and before the Lamb." Revelation 7:9 NIV

48 - Scriptures

Motivate: _____

"For all of you who were baptized into Christ [into a spiritual union with the Christ, the Anointed] have clothed yourselves with Christ [that is, you have taken on His characteristics and values]." Galatians 3:27 AMP

Teach: _____

"Now there were Jews living in Jerusalem, devout and God-fearing men from every nation under heaven. And when this sound was heard, a crowd gathered, and they were bewildered because each one was hearing those in the upper room speaking in his own language or dialect. They were completely astonished, saying, "Look! Are not all of these who are speaking Galileans? Then how is it that each of us hears in our own language or native dialect? [Among us there are] Parthians, Medes and Elamites, and people of Mesopotamia, Judea and Cappadocia, Pontus and Asia [Minor], Phrygia and Pamphylia, Egypt and the districts of Libya around Cyrene, and the visitors from Rome, both Jews and proselytes (Gentile converts to Judaism), Cretans and Arabs—we all hear them speaking in our [native] tongues about the mighty works of God!" Acts 2:5-11 AMP

Win: _____

"And it shall come to pass, that whosoever shall call on the name of the Lord shall be saved." Acts 2:21 KJV

Trust: _____

"There is one body [of believers] and one Spirit—just as you were called to one hope when called [to salvation]—" Ephesians 4:4 AMP

Fear-Not: _____

"And He [that same Jesus] is the propitiation for our sins [the atoning sacrifice that holds back the wrath of God that would otherwise be directed at us because of our sinful nature—our worldliness, our lifestyle]; and not for ours alone, but also for [the sins of all believers throughout] the whole world." 1 John 2:2 AMP

Shift: _____

"Just as each one of you has received a special gift [a spiritual talent, an ability graciously given by God], employ it in serving one another as [is appropriate for] good stewards of God's multi-faceted grace [faithfully using the diverse, varied gifts and abilities granted to Christians by God's unmerited favor]." 1 Peter 4:10 AMP

Devotional # 49

Heart Envy

"Do not let your heart envy sinners, but always be zealous for the fear of the Lord. There is surely a future hope for you, and your hope will not be cut off." Proverbs 23:17-18 NIV

This scripture says it clearly. There are so many times when the lives of those who don't know God seem so much more appealing, fulfilling, and favorable than those who serve God with all their heart. But when all is said and done, the big question remains, "For what shall it profit a man, if he shall gain the whole world, and lose his own soul?" Mark 8:36 KJV.

Some may not think that the lifestyle they live now will affect their future. They get so busy and caught up living in the moment, that the future is a future thought. A child who was led by the wrong company of mischievous friends and fell into the hands of the law, now has a future that is a direct result of their earlier years. Their years of "fun" and "freedom" can never be redone to yield a different result; their lives were stamped and sealed by the law.

Still, there are others whose wayward lives were fortunately not affected by the law; however, one may wonder if their later misfortunes experienced in life, was actually their conviction for such deeds.

Living life undisciplined and unguided, certainly has a way of rewarding us accordingly as we face our latter and more mature years. The bible says "When you were slaves of sin, you were free in regard to righteousness [you had no desire to conform to God's will]. So, what benefit did you get at that time from the things of which you are now ashamed? [None!]" Romans 6:20-21 AMP

There are things we live with every day that remind us of our past choices, back then we were "happy" and "free". "You who are young, be happy while you are young, and let your heart give you joy in the days of your youth. Follow the ways of your heart and whatever your eyes see, but know that for all these things God will bring you into judgment." Ecclesiastes 11:9 NIV

Judgement is certainly a hard pill to swallow. But in all these things, the bible teaches us to "flee youthful passions and pursue righteousness, faith, love, and peace, along with those who call on the Lord from a pure heart." 2 Timothy 2:22 NIV. "Don't let anyone look down on you because you are young, but set an example for the believers in speech, in conduct, in love, in faith and in purity." 1 Timothy 4:12 NIV

When your eyes get a little large with envy, remind yourself that... God has plans for you and your hope will not be cut off.

We don't serve a God that operates on a flashy, pompous mentality. We serve a humble God. A God who is jealous for us. "...for I, the Lord your God, am a jealous God, punishing the children for the sin of the parents to the third and fourth generation of those who hate me, but showing love to a thousand generations of those who love me and keep my commandments." Exodus 20:5-6 NIV.

Isn't God's love worth extending to our generations?

No matter our past, no matter how long the road was to get to God. We can never turn around and redo what was already done; but it is never too late to have our heart renewed and restored. It is never too late to be passionate about the things of God.

No matter your age, exercise your gifts and take joy in them! Do not take your talents for granted. There are promises stored up for you, and God will guide you into your purpose. He will open doors for you into your calling, and he will change the trajectory of your generational future. "There is surely a future hope for you, and your hope will not be cut off." Proverbs 23:18 NIV

49 - Scriptures

Motivate:

"If we confess our sins, he is faithful and just to forgive us our sins and to cleanse us from all unrighteousness." 1 John 1:9 ESV

Teach:

"For it is by grace you have been saved, through faith—and this is not from yourselves, it is the gift of God— not by works, so that no one can boast." Ephesians 2:8-9 NIV

Win:

"Love is patient and kind. Love is not jealous or boastful or proud or rude. It does not demand its own way. It is not irritable, and it keeps no record of being wronged." 1 Corinthians 13:4-5 NLT

Trust:

"For where jealousy and selfish ambition exist, there is disorder [unrest, rebellion] and every evil thing and morally degrading practice." James 3:16 AMP

Fear-Not:

"… neither is the one who plants nor the one who waters anything, but [only] God who causes the growth. He who plants and he who waters are one [in importance and esteem, working toward the same purpose]; but each will receive his own reward according to his own labor. For we are God's fellow workers [His servants working together]; you are God's cultivated field [His garden, His vineyard], God's building." 1 Corinthians 3:7-9 AMP

Shift: _____

"… For as long as there is jealousy and strife and discord among you, are you not unspiritual, and are you not walking like ordinary men [unchanged by faith]?" 1 Corinthians 3:3 AMP

Devotional # 50

Purposeful Love

"If you [only] love those who love you, what credit is that to you? For even sinners love those who love them. If you do good to those who do good to you, what credit is that to you? For even sinners do the same. If you lend [money] to those from whom you expect to receive [it back], what credit is that to you? Even sinners lend to sinners expecting to receive back the same amount. But love [that is, unselfishly seek the best or higher good for] your enemies, and do good, and lend, expecting nothing in return; for your reward will be great (rich, abundant), and you will be sons of the Most High; because He Himself is kind and gracious and good to the ungrateful and the wicked. Be merciful (responsive, compassionate, tender) just as your [heavenly] Father is merciful." Luke 6:32-36 AMP

To be who God wants us to be is a willful act. We choose to humble ourselves to display Christ, to put on his armor and to live in a way that pleases him. It is not unintentional; it is very intentional. We do not follow blindly, the ways of God; We purpose within our hearts to do so wholeheartedly, and we work on it day after day. Love is not only for the deserving, but also for everyone, unselfishly expecting nothing in return. This is the kind of God we serve. A God who is Gracious and Kind and Merciful even when we don't deserve it. A God whose Love is Purposeful.

50 - Scriptures

Motivate: _____

"He who does not love does not know God, for God is love." 1 John 4:8 NKJV

Teach: _____

"If ye love me, keep my commandments." John 14:15 KJV

Win: _____

"And I am convinced that nothing can ever separate us from God's love. Neither death nor life, neither angels nor demons, neither our fears for today nor our worries about tomorrow—not even the powers of hell can separate us from God's love. No power in the sky above or in the earth below—indeed, nothing in all creation will ever be able to separate us from the love of God that is revealed in Christ Jesus our Lord." Romans 8:38-39 NLT

Trust: _____

"But God clearly shows and proves His own love for us, by the fact that while we were still sinners, Christ died for us." Romans 5:8 AMP

Fear-Not: _____

"The Lord hath appeared of old unto me, saying, Yea, I have loved thee with an everlasting love: therefore with lovingkindness have I drawn thee." Jeremiah 31:3 KJV

Shift: _____

"The Lord your God is in your midst, A Warrior who saves. He will rejoice over you with joy; He will be quiet in His love [making no mention of your past sins], He will rejoice over you with shouts of joy." Zephaniah 3:17 AMP

Devotional # 51

With Wisdom & Love

(The Rod)

"He who withholds the rod [of discipline] hates his son, But he who loves him disciplines and trains him diligently and appropriately [with wisdom and love]." Proverbs 13:24 AMP

We've all heard of the old phrase "Spare the rod and spoil the child" (an aphorism generally referring to corporal or physical punishment related to the disciplining of a child), and many have used the phrase interchangeably within Christian based teachings and upbringings for generations. (I encourage you to research the phrase and where it came from). You will find that a quick internet search will reveal that the phrase is not entirely biblically based but rather a sarcastic remark in a poem titled Hudibras that was published in several parts in the 1660's and was immediately successful, appealing to many. It was written from a poet and skeptic, Samuel Butler, who targeted and opposed the extreme religious beliefs in militant Puritanism during a time when they sought to reform the church government throughout the nation.

Discipline, in itself, widely has to do with gaining control. One's first thought in describing discipline might be - to gain control of the undesirable behavior of a person by some sort of punishment in an effort to correct it. It is true that the bible speaks of not withholding the rod of discipline, but this should not be interpreted in the manner of which it was spoken about in the poem by Butler. In the scripture, the bible advises that discipline should be done with wisdom and love. Inflicting physical pain, as some may think the rod symbolizes, is not a depiction of wisdom or love. In fact, many Christians can't even bear the thought of the painful physical punishment Christ Jesus had to endure because of what the people determined was necessary.

Inflicting physical pain drives fear into the heart and mind and serves as a trained trigger to deter one from future actions that would lead to the infliction of pain. Indeed, there are some who believe that such discipline has caused them to be better because they were able to redirect their life to the right path. But there are also those who've endured it and felt it was completely unnecessary, and they went on to harbor unforgiveness in their hearts, causing rebellion, loss of love, loss of genuine joy, loss of respect, and leading to many broken parent-child relationships. Deeper yet, it may cause some to question the faith or religious beliefs of those who justify this behavior, thereby paving the way in latter days, for some who have been deeply afflicted by it, to turn their back on the body of Christ (the church).

When we think of our God holding a rod, there is no fear attached to the thought. Rather the "rod of discipline" is singular possessive and governs 'He' who holds the rod. Therefore, there is comfort found in a Shepherd that is well equipped with a rod that symbolizes that he is a self-controlled protector, guiding our way and extending his staff to pull us up when we fall and not beat us down. That rod, in itself, is the picture of discipline. Not the discipline that the world has made it out to be, but the personal discipline of the disciple themself who holds the rod.

"...I fear no evil, for You are with me; Your rod [to protect] and Your staff [to guide], they comfort and console me." Psalm 23:4 AMP

Not only does 'the rod' symbolize protection, guidance, and comfort, but we see that the Fruit of the Spirit of God is attributable to the character of the disciple who operates in **Wisdom** and **Love** (both Wisdom and Love are interchangeable with who God is).

"But the fruit of the Spirit [the result of His presence within us] is love [unselfish concern for others], joy, [inner] peace, patience [not the ability to wait, but how we act while waiting], kindness, goodness, faithfulness, gentleness, self-control. Against such things there is no law. And those who belong to Christ Jesus have crucified the sinful nature together with its passions and appetites." Galatians 5:22-24 AMP

"But the wisdom from above is first pure [morally and spiritually undefiled], then peace-loving [courteous, considerate], gentle, reasonable [and willing to listen], full of compassion and good fruits. It is unwavering, without [self-righteous] hypocrisy [and self-serving guile]. And the seed whose fruit is righteousness (spiritual maturity) is sown in peace by those who make peace [by actively encouraging goodwill between individuals]." James 3:17-18 AMP.

Whatever rod we are given in life, there is a responsibility attached to the individual in possession, to study to show themselves approved (2 Tim. 2:15). A driver holding the rod of a car must learn to drive and follow instructions. A doctor holding the rod of medical equipment must learn how to operate effectively and follow procedures. A teacher who holds the rod of knowledge and direction must be taught. A shepherd who holds the rod of guiding and protecting the sheep, must learn the qualities of being a good Shepherd. Likewise, when raising God's children, who we are in Christ is essential in disciplining with Wisdom and Love; no less is expected.

51 - Scriptures

Motivate: _____

"But I say, walk habitually in the [Holy] Spirit [seek Him and be responsive to His guidance], and then you will certainly not carry out the desire of the sinful nature [which responds impulsively without regard for God and His precepts]. Galatians 5:16 AMP

Teach: _____

"For the sinful nature has its desire which is opposed to the Spirit, and the [desire of the] Spirit opposes the sinful nature; for these [two, the sinful nature and the Spirit] are in direct opposition to each other [continually in conflict], so that you [as believers] do not [always] do whatever [good things] you want to do." Galatians 5:17 AMP

Win: _____

But if you are guided and led by the Spirit, you are not subject to the Law." Galatians 5:18 AMP

Trust: _____

"Whoever does not love does not know God, because God is love." 1 John 4:8 NIV

Fear-Not: _____

"But the wisdom from above is first pure [morally and spiritually undefiled], then peace-loving [courteous, considerate], gentle, reasonable [and willing to listen], full of compassion and good fruits. It is unwavering, without [self-righteous] hypocrisy [and self-serving guile]. James 3:17 AMP

Shift: _____

"And the seed whose fruit is righteousness (spiritual maturity) is sown in peace by those who make peace [by actively encouraging goodwill between individuals]." James 3:18 AMP.

Devotional # 52

Perfecting Patience

(Part I: Patience and the Will of God)

"Knowing this, that the trying of your faith worketh patience." James 1:3 KJV

The Amplified (AMP) version says that the testing produces endurance, and the English Standard Version (ESV) says that the testing produces steadfastness. Trying is troubles, irritations, and stress; Testing speaks of examining, measure, trial and verification. **This trying and testing produces patience** (the capacity to maintain composure, self-control and tolerance with humility), **endurance** (the ability to persist with strength), and **steadfastness** (unwavering faithfulness). Each in its own right expresses the virtue of what it means to be patient and how to work that patience. This is something that God wants us to grasp and know so that we don't miss the teaching, by getting so caught up in our woes that we end up retaking the tests again and again.

I personally do not like retaking tests, and I don't know anyone who does. I remember trying to study for a multiple-choice test that seemed to contain so much information that I just could not retain everything. I was trying to learn and study at the same time in a very short period, and the information was so much that it was also very easily forgotten. So, what did I do? I used the process of memorization. I took my time and wrote down every possible question along with the answers and memorized all of it and I passed the test with no issues.

Memorization isn't a bad thing but cramming so much information in such a short period of time without full understanding and retention, only has a temporary benefit.

James 1:12 tells us that blessed is the man who endures, who remains steadfast, who perseveres. It's not enough that we only temporarily receive just enough patience that we need for the moment. James 1:4 tells us that patience or endurance should have its perfect work. Meaning that it should be fully matured in us, thorough and complete so that we don't lack anything in that area. And it really is a work, because it is a process of maturing in a world where most people tend to be very impatient. And when we're impatient we can take the wrong steps, make the wrong moves, say the wrong things, do the wrong things, and be at turmoil every step of the way.

Have you ever been through a process where you were just so stressed out that your hair was falling out, or you were stress eating or barely had an appetite; or you just couldn't sleep or get comfortable enough to rest? What about the feeling of uneasiness, irritability, anxiety, or worry? We can even get a bit testy, demanding, edgy, and have short fuse. Those things all come with being impatient.

We've all had those feelings at one point or another; we may have even experienced some of those feelings or emotions today, and let's admit that it comes very naturally and instinctive. It tends to arise from our circumstances, and it dictates our state of mind. But as children of God, we are tasked on daily basis to not let our natural instinctive selves, direct or order our lives in a manner where we are operating outside of the will of God.

The will of God is more than his plans for us. The will of God includes the expression of how we engage the truth of who we are in him based on the abilities and measure he given us (**patience**). The will of God also includes the expression of repeatedly doing and practicing that truth, so that it becomes a habitual behavior (**perfecting patience**) that is rooted in who God says we are and not the instinctive behavior that is natural to the world.

Perfecting Patience

(Part II - Patience, Peace, Wait)

Jesus said a prayer looking up to heaven, in John 17, and as he was speaking to God the father about the disciples or believers in the world, he said in verse 16-20 AMP that "They are not of the world, just as I am not of the world. Sanctify them in the truth [set them apart for Your purposes, make them holy]; Your word is truth. Just as You commissioned and sent Me into the world, I also have commissioned and sent them (believers) into the world. For their sake I sanctify Myself [to do Your will], so that they also may be sanctified [set apart, dedicated, made holy] in [Your] truth. "I do not pray for these alone [it is not for their sake only that I make this request], but also for [all] those who [will ever] believe and trust in Me through their message, that they all may be one; just as You, Father, are in

Me and I in You, that they also may be one in Us, so that the world may believe [without any doubt] that You sent Me."

This truth that fuels the fruit of the Spirit, is the completeness and thorough working of the patience of our Lord which also leads to peace. There will always be the issues of life and continuous burdens that we will lay down and pick up. One may think that being in Christ is a reprieve from those issues and that everything will be seamless without the disturbances that generally occur in life. Or that we can escape those issues just by being who God wants us to be; but that is a naive thought. This may be hard for many to accept (including new Christians or those considering coming to Christ), but even though nothing can ever separate us from Christ's love, [*Does it mean he no longer loves us if we have trouble or calamity, or are persecuted, or hungry, or destitute, or in danger, or threatened with death? (As the Scriptures say, "For your sake we are killed every day; we are being slaughtered like sheep.") No, despite all these things, overwhelming victory is ours through Christ, who loved us.*] Romans 8:35-37 NLT

Therefore, accepting Christ is the easy part, but it doesn't mean that we're receiving an easy life. John 16:33 ESV says "I have said these things to you, that in me you may have peace. In the world you will have tribulation. But take heart; I have overcome the world."

There is a process to become who God wants us to be, as mortals who are connected to the immortality of our spiritual being.

We are spiritual beings because we are a people created **by** God and **of** God, and God **is** a spirit. So, the Peace that the Bible teaches us is not a freedom from disturbance, but rather a spiritual peace that comes through perfecting/mature patience. And that maturity is what helps us to wait on the Lord. We can't wait on the Lord without patience. And in order for the process to be beneficial to us, we need to have peace.

Patience, Peace, and Waiting are all Verbs that work hand in hand. They express some type of action, or happening, or state of being. Patience is action, Peace is happening, Waiting is a state of being that allows our mindset to remain in a place of hope and expectation. These are 3 major aspects of Perfecting Patience; And they all describe the 3 main types of Verbs, which are Action, Linking, and Helping Verbs.

Action (patience) speaks of expressing a process or response while in transition and can also be a shift of possession or ownership of what's being transitioned. Linking (peace) speaks of connecting us (our spirit man) to what is happening to us (in our natural man). This linking closes the gap and allows the truth of God's word and the fruit of his spirit to take precedence through all that he has made us to be. And Helping (waiting) speaks of combining the possibility of expectation and a state of being, to the actions and happenings of our circumstances while in transition.

Believe it or not Helping Verbs (like waiting) are used before action and linking verbs to bring us to a present state of being or state of mind that gives us a reason, an encouragement, and a hope for an expected outcome while we are going through the process, so that we don't lose sight of the goal or the finish line.

Patience is not the only verb of the Spirit of God. So are all the other fruits of his spirit; and Verbs are considered an important element in the eight parts of our Speech. Usually listed as the 3rd part of speech, right after Noun and Pronoun. Verbs describe action and is the main part of the make-up of sentences. Sentences that contain affirmations, statements or basis about a subject. Sentences that are the spoken words of our tongue that has the power to manifest life or death (Proverbs 18:21).

So, whether we are Perfecting Patience or anything we do in life, it begins with **God** (Noun), and it moves by **the Spirit** of God (Pronoun; Every name that refers to the one true God), and it is spoken into existence by the expression of the Word of God (Verb; what God does).

Genesis 1:**1** "In the beginning **God**…" (Noun)

Genesis 1:**2** "And the **Spirit** of God…" (Pronoun)

Genesis 1:**3** "And God said, **Let there be** …" (Verb)

52 - Scriptures

Motivate: _____

"But they that wait upon the Lord shall renew their strength; they shall mount up with wings as eagles; they shall run, and not be weary; and they shall walk, and not faint."(Isaiah 40:31 KJV)

Teach: _____

"All of us who are mature [pursuing spiritual perfection] should have this attitude. And if in any respect you have a different attitude, that too God will make clear to you." Philippians 3:15 AMP

Win: _____

"Rejoice in hope, be patient in tribulation, be constant in prayer." Romans 12:12 ESV

Trust: _____

"But if we hope for what we do not see, we wait for it with patience" Romans 8:25 ESV

Fear-Not: _____

"I have told you these things, so that in Me you may have [perfect] peace. In the world you have tribulation and distress and suffering, but be courageous [be confident, be undaunted, be filled with joy]; I have overcome the world." [My conquest is accomplished, My victory abiding.]" John 16:33 AMP

Shift: _____

"Do not be anxious about anything, but in everything by prayer and supplication with thanksgiving let your requests be made known to God." (Phil. 4:6 ESV)

A Message from the Author

Dear Reader,

Being a Christian, Wife and Mother, has truly grounded me in ways that I could never explain; and I am truly inspired that God has used me in this season, and there is so much more to come.

This is officially my second Devotional book and I'm super excited that you have continued with me on this journey. Since my last book, I've continued to blog on my website www.gmsunshinedevotionals.com, where you can follow and connect with me. I have also had the privilege and opportunity to expound on the devotionals in my first book *'Devotions for a Purposeful Walk'* which eventually paved a path for me to launch my very first Internet Radio Program 'Out of the Heart Flows' through 106inspiration.com powered by 106liveradio.com.

I've also written 2 children's books in a series titled 'Princess Jaleah' (inspired by my oldest daughter) and will soon publish additional children and inspirational books.

I know that this book will be a blessing to you as it has been to me, and I am looking forward to all that God is about to do in the lives of his people. God Bless you.

G.M.

Guest Writer
(Devotional #'s 11 & 12)

Tinasha "Tish" Gray is an ordained Minister of the Gospel, Inspirational Speaker, Wellness Educator, and a Christian Counselor. She is the Founder and CEO of Source of Wellness Ministries, Author of the Source of Wellness book series as well as co-Author of the book 'From Brokenness to Wholeness' (a book written with her husband Jason Gray).

Tinasha is also the CEO and General Manager of 106 Live Radio (106liveradio.com) broadcasting Live from Atlanta Georgia to a global audience. There, she is also a Christian Broadcaster & Host of the 'Tinasha Gray Show' as well as a co-host of 'The Epic Marriage Celebration' (a talk show program for marriages).

Bibliography

Unless otherwise noted, all scripture is taken from the King James Version (KJV) of the Bible (Public Domain in the USA).

Scripture quotations & marked bible versions of KJV, NIV, ESV, NKJV, AMP, and NLT taken from:
- King James Bible. (Public Domain in the USA)
- Holy Bible, New International Version®, NIV® Copyright © 1973, 1978, 1984, 2011 by Biblica, Inc.® Used by permission. All rights reserved worldwide.
- The ESV® Bible (The Holy Bible, English Standard Version®) copyright © 2001 by Crossway Bibles, a publishing ministry of Good News Publishers.
- The Holy Bible, New King James Version, Copyright © 1982 Thomas Nelson. All rights reserved.
- Amplified Bible Copyright © 2015 by The Lockman Foundation. All rights reserved www.lockman.org
- Holy Bible, New Living Translation, copyright © 1996, 2004, 2015 by Tyndale House Foundation. Used by permission of Tyndale House Publishers, Inc., Carol Stream, Illinois 60188. All rights reserved.
- NIV & KJV Side-by-Side Bible
Published by Zondervan www.zondervan.com

Maslow, A. H. (1943). A Theory of Human Motivation. Psychological Review, 50(4), 370-96.

Word Search, Synonyms, and Definitions taken from:
- https://www.google.com/search?
- https://www.thesaurus.com/browse/ ©2019 Dictionary.com, LLC
- Merriam-Webster Online (www.Merriam-Webster.com)
- Merriam-Webster Online Dictionary copyright © 2015 by Merriam-Webster, Incorporated
- Merriam-Webster Online Thesaurus copyright © 2015 by Merriam-Webster, Incorporated

Constitution of the United States of America (1787)
https://billofrightsinstitute.org/primary-sources/constitution
©2022. Bill of Rights Institute

Hudibras/Samuel Butler/Puritanism
©2021 Encyclopædia Britannica, Inc. All Rights Reserved.
https://www.britannica.com/topic/Hudibras-poem-by-Butler
https://www.britannica.com/biography/Samuel-Butler-English-author-1612-1680
https://www.britannica.com/topic/Puritanism

Types of Verbs.
https://www.uvu.edu/writingcenter/docs/handouts/grammar-usage/typesofverbs.pdf

Verbs: Types and Tenses.
https://gato-docs.its.txstate.edu/jcr:f65012ef-9608-4ee0-a0be-9559038bc97c/Verbs-Types%20and%20Tenses.pdf
Source: Ply, Mary Sue, and Donna Haisty Winchell. Bridging the Communication Gap. Scott, Foresman, and Company, 1989. Created by Rebecca Carnes. Revised: Fall 2005.
STUDENT LEARNING ASSISTANCE CENTER (SLAC).
Texas State University-San Marcos